The Peaceful School
MODELS THAT WORK

HETTY van GURP

The Peaceful School
MODELS THAT WORK

HETTY van GURP

PORTAGE &
MAIN PRESS

Portage and Main Press acknowledges the financial support of the Government of Canada through the Book Publishing Industry Development Program (BPIDP) for our publishing activities.

Printed and bound in Canada by Kromar Printing.

02 03 04 05 06 5 4 3 2 1

National Library of Canada Cataloguing in Publication Data

Van Gurp, Hetty.
   The peaceful school

ISBN 1-55379-000-6

   1. School violence—Prevention. 2. Conflict management. I. Title.
LB3013.3V35 2002   371.7'82   C2002-910481-5

Book and cover design: Gallant Design Ltd.
Paper crane illustrations: Jess Dixon
Back cover photograph: Michelle McMinn

PORTAGE & MAIN PRESS

100-318 McDermot Avenue
Winnipeg, Manitoba, Canada R3A 0A2

E-mail: books@peguis.com
Tel: 204.987.3500
Toll free: 1.800.667.9673
Fax: 204.947.0080
Toll free fax: 1.866.734.8477

Everyone needs an unconditional friend.
This book is dedicated to mine—Connie Jacobs.

ContentsContents

Foreword   ix

Preface   xi

Acknowledgments   xiii

Introduction   1

Innovative Practices of Peaceful Schools   15

    Models That Work   17

    Hillside Park Elementary School   19

    O'Connell Drive Elementary School   22

    William King Elementary School   26

    New Germany Elementary School   28

    John MacNeil Elementary School   30

    Kingston Elementary School   32

    Annapolis East Elementary School   46

    R. B. Dickey Elementary School   50

    Sambro Elementary School   51

    Harrietsfield Elementary School   62

    Chebucto Heights Elementary School   64

    Elmsdale District School   65

    St. Joseph Elementary School   67

    East Richmond Education Centre   68

    Bible Hill Central Elementary School   70

    Atlantic Memorial-Terence Bay Elementary School   72

    Bel Ayr Elementary School   75

    Yorkdale Central School   78

    Coral Springs High School   81

    Unity School   83

Peace Pledge   87

Epilogue   89

    From Belgrade to Belfast   91

Appendices   93

    Appendix A: The Peaceful School Planning Document   95

    Appendix B: Student Conferences   102

    Appendix C: Peace Begins With You   103

    Appendix D: "Peace Begins With Me"   108

References   117

ForewordForeword

The Peaceful School: Models That Work, is a guide for educators who are committed to creating a lasting culture of peace within our school communities by pro-actively teaching peace. The book, so ably compiled and written by Hetty van Gurp, is based on the mission of Peaceful Schools International, *"to provide support to schools throughout the world that have declared a commitment to creating and maintaining a culture of peace."* The Peaceful School International model has attracted much positive attention in Canada and abroad.

As Lieutenant Governor of Nova Scotia and as an educator whose interest in the youth of our country is of great importance to me, I am proud that fellow educators from many parts of the world gather in Nova Scotia to participate in the excellent training seminars offered by Peaceful Schools International. These educators take back to the young people in their classrooms and schools worldwide a very positive message that cooperation and compassion are the foundations on which a peaceful world can be built.

As Founding Patron of Peaceful Schools International and a member of the International Advisory Council, I am pleased to add my support to the efforts of Hetty van Gurp, a strong advocate for making a difference.

There is ever-increasing recognition that peace in the classroom will lead to a more peaceful school, a more peaceful community, and, ultimately, a more peaceful world. It is in this spirit that Hetty van Gurp has written her second book, *The Peaceful School: Models That Work.*

The Honourable Myra A. Freeman, O.N.S.
Lieutenant Governor
Province of Nova Scotia

PrefacePreface

At the twenty-eighth session of UNESCO held in Paris in 1995, the General Conference approved the *Declaration and Integrated Framework of Action on Education for Peace, Human Rights and Democracy.*[1] Among the goals outlined by the international group of ministers of education who wrote the Declaration, the following two clearly provide the rationale for the practices described in this book. The Declaration states that the ministers will strive resolutely to:

- base education on principles and methods that contribute to the development of the personality of pupils, students and adults who are respectful of their fellow human beings and determined to promote peace, human rights and democracy

- pay special attention to improving curricula, the content of textbooks, and other educational materials including new technologies, with a view to educating caring and responsible citizens, open to other cultures, able to appreciate the value of freedom, respectful of human dignity and differences, and able to prevent conflicts or resolve them by non-violent means

Section II of the Integrated Framework document outlines the aims of education for peace, human rights, and democracy. Included are:

- The ultimate goal of education for peace, human rights and democracy is the development in every individual a sense of universal values and types of behaviour on which a culture of peace is predicated.

- Education must develop the ability to value freedom and the skills to meet its challenges.

- Education must develop the ability to recognize and accept the values which exist in the diversity of individuals, genders, peoples and cultures and develop the ability to communicate, share and co-operate with others.

- Education must develop the ability of non-violent conflict-resolution.

- Education must cultivate in citizens the ability to make informed choices.

All politics can do is keep us out of war; establishing a lasting peace is the work of education.

—Maria Montessori

---

1. Available online at: www.unesco.org/education/nfsunesco/pdf/REV_74_E.PDF

Be the change you want to see in the world.

—Gandhi

Advocating the need to educate for peace, human rights, and democracy is a noble undertaking. Teachers rarely need convincing that it is important to do so. However, to move from acknowledging these principles to generating practical applications in the classroom is often challenging.

The purpose of this book is to offer practical ideas and strategies to animate documents such as the UNESCO Declaration. It is my hope that the ideas that follow will inspire you to come up with your own plan to create a school-wide culture of peace. We must teach our young people the attitudes, knowledge, and skills to live well together.

AcknowledgmentsAcknowledgments

As an educator, I often dreamed of working in a school with an ethos so positive that it is evident to anyone entering the front doors—an ethos in which all staff are engaged in promoting an atmosphere of care and respect and in which students, staff, and parents feel secure, welcome, and valued. However, it was not until after the death of my son Ben—following a school bullying incident—that I began to actively pursue my dream. At that time my younger son, Joe, was eleven years old. Even at a young age, Joe frequently encouraged me to put my dreams into action. Today, he continues to be my muse. Recently, Joe embarked on his final year of university studies in electrical engineering. When I asked him about his goals for the coming year, he responded: "I would like to become a better person."

Thank you, Joe, for your inspiration.

I gratefully acknowledge the many teachers and students who so generously allowed me to share their ideas and initiatives. I can only take credit for collecting and assembling the innovative work that is described in this book.

I also wish to thank Leigh Hambly: an editor extraordinaire.

Introduction

INTRODUCTION

CHILDREN'S PEACE TREATY

We the children of the world

declare peace on the future.

We want a planet free of war and weapons.

We want an end to disease,

death and destruction.

Hatred and hunger and homelessness

make no sense to us.

We want them done away with.

Our earth gives food enough for all—

We will share it.

Our skies give us rainbows everywhere—

We will keep them clear.

We want to laugh together, play together,

work together, learn from each other,

explore and improve life for everyone.

We are for peace, now and forever, for all.

— Written by school children in Northern Ireland

Why Must We Teach Peace?

In many parts of the world, there is growing public concern about youth crime and violence. Although statistical evidence indicates that youth crime is decreasing in Canada,[1] many fear that the incidents that do occur are more serious than in the past. In 1995, the Nova Scotia Department of Education surveyed every grade-eight student in the province and found that over 33 percent felt unsafe in school. This is an alarming statistic. Young people have a right to feel safe, if nowhere else, then surely within our schools.

These words of Marian Wright Edelman, founder and president of the Children's Defense Fund, are testimony to the status of many North America children.

> Never have we exposed children so early and relentlessly to cultural messages glamorizing violence, sex, possessions, alcohol and tobacco with so few mediating influences from responsible adults. Never have we experienced such a numbing and reckless reliance on violence to solve problems, feel powerful, or be entertained. Never have so many children been permitted to rely on guns and gangs rather than parents, neighbors and religious congregations and schools for protection and guidance. Never have we pushed so many children on to the tumultuous sea of life without the life vests of nurturing families and communities, caring schools, challenged minds, job prospects and hope (Roberts & Amidon 1999: 171).

Educators, naturally, have an inherent desire to provide a learning environment that is harmonious and safe for all. However, peace cannot be achieved simply by wishing for it, writing tough policies, or mandating it. Accordingly, more and more school communities are looking for ways to foster a lasting culture of peace. What they are finding is this: to create a culture of peace within our school communities, *we must teach peace*.

It is crucial that we educate our youth to live peacefully together as caring, compassionate students in a school community—and as citizens of the world. For despite prodigious efforts, communities throughout the world continue to struggle with the challenge of finding effective ways to erode longstanding patterns of conflict and violence. Certainly, our youth will be

---

1. "Over recent years, there has been an overall decrease in youth crime. In 1997, rates were down 23% from 1991." Fact Sheet, Department of Justice, Canada. Research & Statistics Division.

no more successful than we have been at living peacefully if we merely repeat how commendable peace is or impose peace. Strict adherence to laws, proclamations, and policies is, at best, an uneasy and tenuous submission to peace. We need to actively teach skills and model peaceful ways of learning and living together.

A New Vision

I believe we need a new vision for schools—one that includes educating both the heart and the mind. We want our children and youth to be critical thinkers, creative, and concerned citizens. We want them to understand their responsibility to work together to create a better world for all of us. We want them to treasure their talents, become independent adults with meaningful vocations, appreciate the value of family and friends, and embrace healthy lifestyles.

Educators devote a great deal of time and resources to developing emerging curricula and public school programs. Academically, we know what we want, and we have plenty of ideas and strategies to achieve our goals. Despite dreary media proclamations of student ineptitude, many of our youth are highly articulate and literate. They can, for example, perform mathematical wizardry, and they have an ability to navigate the Internet with astonishing facility. However, in our endeavor to equip youth with what we believe to be essential skills, knowledge, and information, most of us continue to neglect the most important skill—how to live well together. We need to re-examine the priorities of what we teach. Young people need to know and practice the fundamental concepts—equality, justice, human rights, and diversity—that underpin the peace we seek.[2]

Teaching Peace

Peace is a complex matter. The mere presence of quiet acquiescence does not assure peacefulness. We cannot leave the development of understanding and practicing peaceful ways of living together to chance. Young people need to learn "lessons in living"—the skills essential to reducing conflict and violence. "Lessons in living" encompass peace education, the development of emotional intelligence, conflict resolution, environmental awareness, and community service.

I mention "lessons in living" in *Peace in the Classroom* (Winnipeg, MB: Peguis Publishers, 1994). Shortly after its publication, I began visiting neighboring schools and, eventually, schools throughout Nova Scotia. I believed then, and still do, that we need to foster a culture of peace within our schools. This can only be done by teaching each classroom of students lessons in cooperation, effective communication, celebrating diversity, expressing emotions, and resolving conflict creatively. Change begins in the classroom.

2. This paragraph is adapted from a speech given by Glynis Ross to the Nova Scotia School Board Association in May 2000. Used with permission.

The Peaceful School: Models That Work

Teaching "lessons in living" at the elementary level can be accomplished in a number of ways. Some teachers plan lessons and fit them into the weekly timetable. Some infuse "lessons in living" into daily curriculum while others use "teachable moments" to introduce peacemaking skills. No matter what the approach, time can easily be found at the elementary level. At the secondary level, this becomes more of a challenge. Stringent time constraints combined with the need to fulfill curriculum and credit requirements seem to prohibit secondary educators from doing things differently.

From Peaceful Classrooms to a Peaceful School

Since the early 1990s, I have visited dozens of schools that have committed to and sustained a culture of peace. Staff, students, and parents at each school create a place where people want to be. They then work diligently to maintain such an environment. I have been inspired by each one of them.

Over the past ten years, I have also presented peace workshops to hundreds of school staff members. During my presentation, I invite participants to imagine they work in a school called Shangra La:

Imagine

Imagine you are a staff member at Shangra La Community School. Its reputation is so positive that you are inundated with requests from parents asking for special permission to enroll their children in your school. Visitors come from far and near to see for themselves what makes your school unique.

Recently, your principal was interviewed on a national television show. Tomorrow, a journalist is coming to Shangra La to write a feature article about your school. What will the journalist see? What will the journalist hear? What is it that makes Shangra La unique?

I then ask the workshop participants to describe the characteristics that make Shangra La so special. The participants soon discover that the qualities that make Shangra La the celebrated school it is are not unique. They are found in schools that are committed to:

- building healthy relationships

- communicating with understanding and respect

- valuing the input and efforts of each individual

- striving for an appreciation of diversity

A culture of peace will be achieved when the citizens of the world understand global problems; have the skills to resolve conflict constructively; know and live by international standards of human rights, gender and racial equality; appreciate cultural diversity; and respect the integrity of the Earth. Such learning cannot be achieved without intentional, sustained and systematic education for peace.

—Peace Matters, Newsletter of The Hague Appeal for Peace, January 2000

I have come to a frightening conclusion. I am the decisive element in the classroom. It is my personal approach that creates the climate. It is my daily mood that makes the weather. As a teacher I possess tremendous power to make a child's life miserable or joyous. I can be a tool of torture or an instrument of inspiration. I can humiliate or humor, hurt or heal. In all situations it is my response that decides whether a crisis will be escalated or de-escalated, and a child humanized or de-humanized.

—Haim G. Ginott

- creating an environment in which students feel free to express themselves without risk
- ensuring that students are free from intimidation, harassment, and aggression of any kind

From the hundreds of responses I have collected, I have concluded that creating a culture of peace within a school has far more to do with attitude than with resources. The following list reflects ideas and themes consistently deemed essential by teachers, parents, administrators, school bus drivers, secretaries, caretakers, and students:

- individual differences are accepted by all
- students work cooperatively
- staff shares a common vision
- community is highly involved
- "Golden Rule" is taught
- student work is on display
- students are taught positive social skills
- teachers share ideas and materials
- visitors feel welcome
- a good relationship exists between staff and administration
- gender issues are addressed
- students and staff are involved in community outreach initiatives
- yelling is not allowed
- student leadership is encouraged
- all classes are involved in school-wide themes
- discipline policy is developed with input from all
- nutritious food is available in cafeteria
- respect for all by all is obvious
- consequences are fair, consistent, and natural
- an active peer mediation program exists
- the playground is adequately supervised
- students and staff are proud of their school
- problems are dealt with expeditiously

A Global Network of Peaceful Schools

By the late 1990s, I realized there existed neither a system of support nor a means of recognizing the achievements of schools committed to peace. As a result of this observation, in 1998, Don MacLeod, Frank MacCormick, and I established the League of Peaceful Schools, in Nova Scotia. Since then, the League of Peaceful Schools has also been firmly established in Saskatchewan under the auspices of the Public Legal Education Association (PLEA).

The League of Peaceful Schools

The League of Peaceful Schools provides schools with a means of sharing challenges and successes through a newsletter, an annual conference, and training for educators, students, and parents. Judging by the number of schools that have applied for membership, there is a need for such an organization. Many of the innovative practices (starting on page 15) are examples of the exemplary work being done in some of these schools.

Peaceful Schools International

The rapid growth of the League of Peaceful Schools convinced me that schools internationally would also appreciate such a network of support. In 2001, I devoted several months to traveling to Japan, Cambodia, Serbia, and Macedonia. As I traveled, it became clear to me that schools everywhere *do* share a common vision. It also became evident that educators in these countries are eager for ideas, strategies, and materials to help them promote harmony and understanding within their schools. Educators around the world often work in isolation, reinventing programs and initiatives that have been established successfully elsewhere.

It is good to have an end to journey towards, but it is the journey that matters in the end.

—Ursula LeGuin

It was from these realizations that Peaceful Schools International (PSI) was conceived. PSI is an organization that provides support and recognition to schools that have declared a commitment to creating and maintaining a culture of peace. The criteria for membership in PSI were developed from responses from educators and students to the "Shangra La" activity in the countries I visited. These criteria are not intended as a rigid checklist; they offer general guiding principles that schools are encouraged to follow as guideposts in their journey. The journey is unique in each school. As an organization, PSI is analogous to the stone in the classic folktale, *Stone Soup* (see page 10). PSI encourages schools to formulate their own special blend of "ingredients" in creating a culture of peace.

STONE SOUP

There once was a man who had been traveling for a long time. Having run out of food, he was weary and hungry from his journey. When he came upon a small village, he thought, "Maybe someone could share some food."

When the man knocked at the first house, he asked the woman who answered, "Could you spare a bit of food? I've traveled a long way and am very hungry."

"I'm sorry, but I have nothing to give you," the woman replied.

So the traveler went to the next door and asked again. The answer was the same. He went from door to door, and each time he was turned away.

But then one villager said, "All I have is some water."

"Thank you," the traveler said, smiling gratefully. "We can make some soup from that water. We can make stone soup."

He asked the man for a cooking pot and started building a small fire. As the water started to boil, a passing villager stopped and asked him what he was doing. "I'm making stone soup," the traveler replied. "Would you like to join me?" The curious villager agreed.

"First, we must add a special stone," said the traveler. "One with magic in it." He reached into his knapsack and carefully unwrapped a special stone he'd been carrying with him for many years. Then he put it in the simmering pot.

Soon people from the village heard about this strange man who was making soup from a stone. They started gathering around the fire, asking questions. "What does your stone soup taste like?" asked one of the villagers.

"Well, it would be better with a few onions," the traveler admitted.

"Oh, I have some onions," the villager replied.

Another villager said, "I could bring a few carrots."

Someone else offered, "We still have some potatoes in our garden. I'll go get them."

One by one, each villager brought something to add to the pot. What had started as just some water and a magic stone had now become a delicious soup, enough to feed the whole village. The traveler and the villagers sat down together to enjoy their feast and the miracle they helped create.

Never doubt that you can make a difference…

Never doubt that a small group of committed individuals can change the world; indeed, it's the only thing that ever does.

—Margaret Mead

PSI Membership Criteria

- A collaborative approach to school-based decision making

  Parent input is valued, staff members work together as a team, and there is a high level of participation in school decision making and goal-setting. There is an expectation that everyone on staff can and must make a difference in the overall life of the school.

  All staff members share their wide range of expertise willingly, and both successes and problems are shared.

  As in all organizations, when people are invited to be actively involved in decision making, a climate of cooperation, support, and understanding emerges. Fostering a spirit of mutual respect and inclusion in decision making plays an important role in the ever-increasing challenges that face schools in all parts of the world.

- Curricular and/or extracurricular peace education initiatives[3]

  Many books and other resource materials are available that contain innovative, practical lessons in cooperation, respecting differences, communicating effectively, expressing emotions in a positive manner, and resolving conflict creatively and nonviolently. No single book or program will meet everyone's needs. With a variety of resources made available in the school, teachers are free to use those that are relevant to the needs of their students—needs that vary from year to year.

  In some schools and school districts, peace education has been incorporated into curricular activities. Social studies, health, and language arts are some of the subject areas that are conducive to such integration. In other schools and school districts, peace education activities are introduced in an extracurricular manner. For example, many schools host peace festivals, invite guest speakers, and hold assemblies with a focus on peace. *How* peace education occurs is not as important as the fact that it *does* occur.

- Teaching methods that stress participation, cooperation, problem solving, and respect for differences

  The days of passive learning have all but disappeared. In many parts of the world, students are being encouraged to work cooperatively with one another and to take an active role in their own learning.

  Discussions, small-group work, cooperative learning, and attention to individual needs all contribute to a classroom environment in which students feel free to take risks without fear of failure.

---

3. Peace education, as defined by the Canadian International Development Agency (CIDA), is seen as: "…activities that promote the knowledge, skills and attitudes that will allow people of all ages, and at all levels, to develop the behaviour changes that can prevent the occurrence of conflict, resolve conflict peacefully, or create the social conditions conducive to peace." *Education and Peacebuilding: A Preliminary Framework*, Canada/CIDA.

We need to encourage students to be critical thinkers, creative, and capable of solving problems as members of a team—characteristics that are not often found in a classroom where students passively listen without opportunities to participate. On the other hand, creative, independent thinking flourishes in an environment where students make choices and where differences in learning rates and styles are acknowledged and celebrated.

In peaceful schools, children are encouraged to be open minded and accepting of others who may look different, have different customs, or hold beliefs that do not correspond with their own. Teachers are focusing more and more on the importance of such understanding and acceptance as a means of creating harmony in the classroom—and in society at large.

■ Student- and community-centered conflict resolution strategies such as peer mediation

When students are taught to become responsible for their own choices and behavior, they are provided with a variety of ways to deal with conflict in a nonviolent manner. From peer mediation to talking circles, peace tables and class meetings to restorative justice forums, a variety of proactive responses to conflict can be introduced through classroom activities, in the school discipline policy, and as the overall approach within the school.

When conflict resolution is implemented—both as part of the curriculum and as a lifestyle to be lived by both adults and youth—respect, tolerance, and community building become "the way we do things around here." Implementation of a conflict resolution program can help schools create their governance structures, develop policies, identify goals, and make curriculum decisions.

■ Community service projects

As we spend more time encouraging our youth to become caring and compassionate citizens, it makes sense that we offer them opportunities to put these principles into action. Many schools organize school-wide or class-based community service projects that address student-identified needs. Often the goals and activities of these projects are woven into or drawn from curricular objectives.

In its broad interpretation, community service can take place anywhere. In many schools, older students read with younger students. The collection of food, clothing, school supplies, and first-aid items for those in need occurs in schools everywhere. Whatever the initiative or project, when students are encouraged to help others, they learn vital lessons in empathy, understanding, and goodwill.

- Opportunities for professional development for all staff focused on creating a positive school climate

As the staff of a school grows and/or changes, the vision of the school and the means by which it is being achieved need to be clearly articulated to new staff members. In addition, all staff members benefit from ongoing opportunities for professional development related to enhancing school climate. There are many advantages to including all staff members in professional development sessions. Everyone in the school community who interacts with the students should be included—from the bus drivers to the playground duty supervisors. Before planning staff development sessions, survey staff members about their interests and needs. This should be done annually as the school culture evolves.

In many schools, parents and community members are given opportunities to attend similar workshops with a focus on family relationships and interactions. These sessions are usually organized by school staff and may be presented by staff or by guests who have a level of expertise in a particular area.

Regional offices of Peaceful Schools International are being established globally. From these offices, schools that become members of PSI receive support in professional development, print materials (including the newsletter, *Peace Talks International*), networking opportunities with other "peaceful schools," workshops, conferences, and any additional and individualized support requested. PSI also assists schools in locating both the human resource experts and curricular materials they need to work toward the realization of their goals.

Schools are encouraged to apply for membership in PSI at any time. Naturally, each school has its own time line. Some schools achieve their goal within a relatively short time frame. Other schools work diligently for three to four years before they feel a celebration of success is in order.

When a school has met the membership criteria, a flag and a membership certificate are presented to the staff and students at a school-wide assembly. For many schools, this event is one of significance to the entire school community and may include a program highlighting student performances, and words of congratulations from community leaders amidst an overall spirit of pride and celebration.

The Peaceful School

The peaceful school is easy to identify. Everyone—educator, student, support staff—exhibits signs and symptoms of inner peace. Here are some behaviors to watch for:

1. The tendency to think and act spontaneously, rather than from fear based upon past experiences.

2. An unmistakable ability to enjoy each moment.

3. Loss of interest in interpreting the actions of others.

4. Loss of interest in judging other people.

5. Loss of interest in judging self.

6. Loss of interest in conflict.

7. Frequent overwhelming episodes of appreciation.

8. Contented feelings of being connected with others and with nature.

9. Frequent episodes of smiling through the eyes from the heart.

10. Increasing tendency to let things happen, rather than make them happen.

11. Increased susceptibility to love extended by others, as well as the uncontrollable urge to extend it.

Innovative Practices
of Peaceful Schools

INNOVATIVE
PRACTICES

Models That Work

An ever growing number of schools have declared a commitment to creating a culture of peace. In each of these schools, the umbrella of peace education embraces many activities, programs, and policies. Striving to create and maintain a culture of peace becomes a way of being. As we foster an ethos of peace by focusing on the development of emotional intelligence, the learning process is enhanced for all students.

The following letter, from Dale Armstrong, principal of Shannon Park School in Dartmouth, Nova Scotia, describes what we often feel in schools committed to a culture of peace.

> As a member of the League of Peaceful Schools, we have endeavored to espouse and live the philosophy of peaceful living. While it takes many shapes, we have found there is no quick fix nor is there any single one "program" that will teach the children responsibility and respect. At our school, we have peer mediation, student leadership, kids making morning and birthday announcements, a new school logo and slogan, peer tutoring, *Peace in the Classroom, Working it Out* (Lion's Quest), 2nd Step and resources too numerous to mention. Also, several teachers have "adopted" students (unbeknownst to them). However, given this framework of support, we have found one avenue that is more empowering that we ever thought possible. That is Music and the Arts. Through our bi-weekly school assemblies, our concerts and our spring productions, our students have learned more about themselves and each other than we could ever teach them in a traditional classroom/school setting. We have invested in our students in a way that allows them to stretch, grow and move outside the parameters. Through African drumming, singing, acting, dancing, performing, practicing, listening as an audience, our students are learning self-discipline, self-direction, trust and mutual respect. They have become more caring and supportive of each other—they are willing to take risks in areas that otherwise would be uncomfortable. They have planted flowers (that no one trampled on), they have painted with a Nova Scotia College of Art and Design student and their work is framed and displayed. The older students work harmoniously (and willingly) with our younger ones.

Relationships are being built among students, and between students and staff. I am so very proud of this school, the students and the teachers who are investing in kids—we are coming together as a community of learners. It is energizing.

In this section, I describe innovative initiatives and projects, and exemplary practices, developed by educators and students in some of the schools I have visited. The ideas of these educators and students deserve to be celebrated and shared with other schools setting out on a similar journey of peace.

Hillside Park Elementary School

15 Hillside Avenue
Lower Sackville, Nova Scotia
B4C 1W6 • 902-864-6873

Hillside Park Elementary has established, over the past several years, a far-reaching reputation for its groundbreaking work with arts infusion, critical pedagogy, and community outreach. Evidence of its commitment to creating a peaceful climate is reflected in the artwork on the walls, the expressions on the faces of the students walking down the halls, and in the interactions between students and staff. Hillside is truly a peaceful school.

Living Gently Together

In the staff room, evidence of a recent professional development session is found on a bulletin board. Staff members have generated ideas to enhance an already peaceful school climate. Ideas include:

- Explore other cultures: dress, customs, lifestyles, food, songs, art, and so on.
- Emphasize the creatures that share the earth with us.
- Use puppets to role-play manners, consideration, and courtesies that smooth the path for all.
- Have children generate words related to friendship and gentle living.
- Pick a word each day, and encourage behaviors that exemplify the meaning of that word.
- Teach manners, and put them into practice each day.
- Show videos of classes engaged in peaceful activities.
- Take photos of students engaged in meaningful activities.
- Play peaceful songs, read poems on the P.A.
- Incorporate math skills in a mystery grid journey to a "peaceful place."
- Use imagery: darken the room and read "peaceful" literature.
- **Peace News**: collect stories, poems, news clips about peaceful living.
- **Peace Journal**: keep individual or class records of acts of kindness.
- **Gratitude Day**: express gratitude for everyday things through discussion, writing, art, and so on.
- **Peaceful Living**: write fables related to common difficulties in getting along with others.
- Plan, plant, and care for a "Peace Garden."

Hillside Town Hall

Every three weeks, students, staff, parents, and guardians gather in the gym for a "town hall" meeting. The meeting opens with a lively rendition of the song "Peace Is," followed by a declaration of the "World Pledge." Town hall meetings provide opportunities for students to discuss issues of importance to them and to share poetry, prose, and song. The meetings also strengthen the bond between the school and the Hillside community.

World Pledge

I pledge allegiance to the world,
To cherish every living thing,
To care for earth and sea and air,
With peace and freedom everywhere.

—Lillian Genser

14 Days in December

My visit coincided with preparations for Hillside's third annual celebration of "14 Days in December: Gentle Ways Are Best" (see page 21). On the first of December, a peace package is sent to each family. The package contains a schedule of events for the fourteen days, a length of purple ribbon, and a peace candle. The ribbon is symbolic and can be tied around the candle or worn. The families light the candle each day for two weeks, and they take time to think about how to live together gently—how to be peaceful, kind, concerned, and thoughtful.

Families are also encouraged to plan and work together on a poster, picture, or peace recipe that portrays their ideas about gentle and peaceful living. These efforts are then displayed in the school gym at the Peace and Christmas concert. During these two weeks in December, students also bring in photographs of their families for a collage that celebrates the diversity of Hillside families.

Radio P.E.A.C.E.

Students host "Radio P.E.A.C.E." broadcasts during the first two weeks in December. The broadcasts are aired in the morning. Students make suggestions about acts of kindness, and those who are kind and helpful are recognized.

In February, the radio station changes its broadcast name to "Radio L.O.V.E." Students write poems, organize contests, share news items, read peaceful sportscasts, and so on.

"14 DAYS IN DECEMBER":
GENTLE WAYS ARE BEST

On November 17, 1997, the YMCA of Greater Halifax/Dartmouth awarded its annual Peace Medal to TRIAC, an organization in Eastern Halifax County that promotes peace, for its initiative: "14 Days in December."

"14 Days in December" was conceived to commemorate the fourteen women who died violently on December 6, 1989, in Montreal. It evolved out of discussions by a committee comprised of educators, law enforcement officers, health care providers, clergy, business persons, and retired persons in the Halifax County East area. This committee, Tri-Community Inter-Agency Council (TRIAC), focused on the violence families suffer in society today and committed to developing approaches to promote nonviolent living within the county's communities. Since the birth of this unique concept in 1992, the celebration has become an important annual event, and its impact has not gone unnoticed. The YMCA's Statement of Peace declares:

> Peace has many dimensions. It is not only a state of relationships among nations. We cannot expect to live in a world of peace if we are unable to live in peace with those close to us—even those who differ from us...

> The responsibility for peace begins with each person, in relationship with family and friends, and extends to community life and national activities. There are no simple recipes...

The organizers of "14 Days in December" accepted the responsibility for promoting peace throughout their community, and they deserve to be recognized and celebrated as role models for us all.

The goals of this project are:

■ To effect change of attitudes and promote discussion and awareness of all forms of violence in the daily lives of individuals, families, and social structures.

■ To educate individuals, families, community groups, the school system, businesses, and the health-care sector on the importance of both individual and collective efforts to promote peace and nonviolent living.

■ To promote alternatives to destructive learned behavior and involve the people of the community, hopefully leaving them with a renewed sense of empowerment and tools to continue in the direction of change and a zero tolerance for all forms of violence and abuse.

Strategies developed to meet these goals are as diverse and creative as the individuals involved. Some examples of these ideas are:

■ Tree lighting ceremonies in each of the communities involved (on December 1)

■ A community quilt project

■ Dinner theatre

■ Puppet show

■ Raffles (with proceeds for women's shelter)

■ Posters created by students

■ T-shirts with "14 Days..." slogan

■ Peace conferences in local schools

■ Family candle-lighting

■ Peace Park for families to enjoy

The organizers hope that "14 Days in December" will continue to be an annual event and will become contagious. Their wish is to see an epidemic of peace in homes throughout communities everywhere.

O'Connell Drive Elementary School

40 O'Connell Drive
Porter's Lake, Nova Scotia
B3E 1E8 • 902-827-4112

"14 Days in December"

Like Hillside, O'Connell Drive Elementary also celebrates "14 Days in December." All students learn about "Sadako and the Peace Cranes,"[1] and the entire school population makes origami paper cranes that are displayed in the lobby. (See pages 23-25 for instructions.) During "14 Days in December," students can earn Sadako (**S**incere **A**cts and **D**eeds of **A**ctual **K**indness at **O**'Connell) awards. Anyone—teacher or student—can nominate someone for doing a kind act or deed. Everyone who is nominated receives an award.

Each day, peaceful music is played through the P.A. system after recess, and students are asked to reflect upon kind and caring things they have done or have witnessed. As well, children play the role of "Secret Angel"— they carry out acts of kindness for another child in the school.

Co-Co the Peace Bear

Students are encouraged to think and write about peace, friendship, and understanding. During the school year, Co-Co the Peace Bear periodically visits classrooms and collects students' writing, which he keeps in his knapsack. He also participates in special events and assemblies. In fact, Co-Co was introduced to the students at a school assembly:

> Co-Co goes from class to class to encourage peace in our school. In each class, people give him poems or stories on peace. When he comes to your classroom, you should treat him with respect. He is not just a teddy bear. He is a symbol of friendship. This year, to see how much writing he gets, we will display it in the gym for all to see. The more he gets, the more we know how hard people are trying to encourage peace in our school. Co-Co is here to remind us that peace, friendship, and understanding are awesome. Keep thinking of great ideas and have fun!

Peace Things

*There is a bird,
that is a dove.
It's a peace dove.
There is a flower,
that is a poppy.
It's a peace flower.
There is a world,
that can be a peaceful
world, if everybody tries.*

—Rebecca

---

1. See *Sadako and the Thousand Paper Cranes* by Eleanor Coerr.

HOW TO FOLD
A PAPER CRANE

1. Begin with a square piece of paper—ideally, one side colored and the other side plain. Place the colored side face up on the table. (In all diagrams, the shaded part represents the colored side.)

2. Fold diagonally to form a triangle. Be sure the points line up. Make all creases very sharp. You can even use your thumbnail. Important: Unfold the paper!

3. Now fold the paper diagonally in the opposite direction, forming a new triangle.

4. Unfold the paper and turn it over so the white side is up. The dotted lines in the diagram are creases you have already made.

5. Fold the paper in half to the "east" to form a rectangle. Unfold the paper.

6. Fold the paper in half to the "north" to form a new rectangle.

7. Unfold the rectangle, but don't flatten it out. Your paper will have the creases shown by the dotted lines in the figure below.

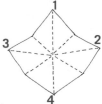

8. Bring all four corners of the paper together, one at a time. This will fold the paper into the flat square shown below. This square has an open end where all four corners of the paper come together. It also has two flaps on the right and two flaps on the left.

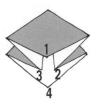

9. Lift the upper right flap, and fold in the direction of the arrow. Crease along line a-c.

10. Lift the upper left flap, and fold in the direction of the arrow. Crease along line a-b.

11. Lift the paper at point d (see previous diagram) and fold down the triangle b-d-c. Crease along the line b-c.

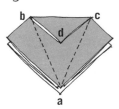

12. Undo the three folds you just made (steps 9, 10, and 11), and your paper will have the crease lines shown here (dotted lines).

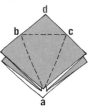

13. Lift just the top layer of the paper at point a. Think of this as opening a frog's mouth. Open it up and back to line b-c. Crease the line b-c inside the frog's mouth.

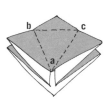 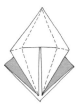

14. Press on points b and c to reverse the folds along lines a-b and a-c. The trick is to get the paper to lie flat in the long diamond shape shown here. At first, it will seem impossible. Have patience.

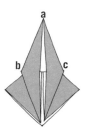

15. Turn the paper over. Repeat steps 9 to 12 on this side. When you have finished, your paper will look like this diamond with the two "legs" at the bottom.

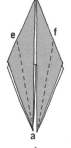

16. Taper the diamond at its legs by folding the top layer of each side in the direction of the arrows along lines a-f and a-e so they meet at the center line.

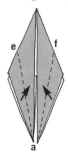

17. Flip the paper over. Repeat step 16 on this side to complete the tapering of the two legs.

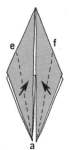

18. This figure has two skinny legs. Lift the upper flap at point f (be sure it's just the upper flap), and fold it over in the direction of the arrow—as if turning the page of a book. This is called a "book fold."

19. Flip the entire figure over. Repeat this "book fold" (step 18) on this side. Be sure to fold over only the top "page."

© 1993 Teaching Tolerance, Montgomery, AL. Adapted from instructions by Informed Democracy. Used by permission.

20. This figure looks like a fox with two pointy ears at the top and a pointy nose at the bottom. Open the upper layer of the fox's mouth at point a, and crease it along line g-h so the fox's nose touches the top of the fox's ears.

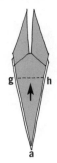

21. Turn the figure over. Repeat step 20 on this side so that all four points touch.

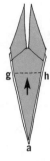

22. Now for another "book fold": Lift the top layer (at point f), and fold it in the direction of the arrow.

23. Flip the entire figure over. Repeat the "book fold" (step 22) on this side.

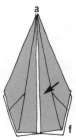

24. There are two points, a and b, below the upper flap. Pull out each one, in the direction of the arrows, as far as shown. Press down along the base (at points x and y) to make them stay in place.

25. Take the end of one of the points, and bend it down to make the head of the crane. Using your thumbnail, reverse the crease in the head, and pinch it to form the beak. The other point becomes the tail.

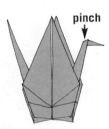

26. Open the body by blowing into the hole underneath the crane, and then gently pulling out the wings. And there it is!

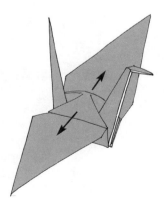

© 1993 Teaching Tolerance, Montgomery, AL. Adapted from instructions by Informed Democracy. Used by permission.

William King Elementary School

91 St. Paul's Avenue
Herring Cove, Nova Scotia
B3V 1H6 • 902-479-4200

Peaceful Living Award

Gerard MacNeil, a grade-five teacher, developed an innovative challenge for upper elementary students. He encourages students to photograph people taking part in "peaceful living" activities—using a camera and film donated by a local photographer. The photographs cover a wide range of activities deemed by students to portray peaceful living; for example, playing a musical instrument, gardening, working on a hobby.

Near the end of the school year, a Peaceful Living Award is presented to two or three students whose photographs best represent peaceful living.

A portion of a mural painted by grade-three students. The mural was displayed on one of the school walls.

Words of Wisdom for Peacekeepers

A few years ago, I was invited to deliver the after-dinner address to a graduating class at the Lester B. Pearson Canadian International Peacekeeping Training Centre located in Clementsport, Nova Scotia. Feeling somewhat out of my element, I appealed to the primary students at William King, where I was the principal at the time, for help. I asked these five-year-olds to give me some advice that I could pass along to the peacekeepers at the Pearson Peacekeeping Centre. Their Words of Wisdom are now displayed on the walls at the centre.

Words of Wisdom for Peacekeepers

- Make sure you don't make any deals so you won't join sides.
- Be careful, because in a war, even the people on the good team could get hurt.
- Run away and when the coast is clear, come out and help. If you can't run fast, use a jeep.
- Always bring a guard with you.
- Talk it out. They might listen if you are peaceful.
- When a gun shoots, duck.
- Give the job to somebody else.
- Hide behind a rock or a tree or a haystack.
- Watch out for swinging swords.
- Don't bring guns into countries.
- Plant flowers.
- Keep up the good work.

New Germany Elementary School

150 School Street
New Germany, Nova Scotia
B0R 1E0 • 902-644-5020

Voices Are Not For Violence

Under the leadership of principal David Ferns, students and staff pledge to try not to use their voices for violence. The voice is not often considered to be a source of violence, but all teachers and most students know that name-calling and verbal bullying regularly precede physical violence.

Students and staff devised a pledge to raise awareness of verbal abuse. The Campaign Pledge (see page 29) was taken by all members of the Southwest Regional School Board, the president of the Nova Scotia Teachers' Union, the senior management of the board, and by every student at the school. The hope is that various churches, volunteer agencies, and labor unions in the area (such as bus drivers) will also take the pledge.

That which we are, we shall teach.

—Emerson

Students in many classes repeat the pledge each day. Others graph the use of verbal violence on favorite TV programs and movies. Still others write letters to celebrities and sports heroes to ask them to take the pledge. The school drama club wrote a play around the theme and performed it for the school and the school board.

The provincial Legislature voted an unanimous motion of congratulations to the school for its work. The members of the House of Assembly have also been challenged by the students to take the pledge, a difficult thing for those whose stock in trade is embarrassing the opposition or "putting down" anyone from a different party.

Every day in the classroom, students who have taken the pledge are awarded a badge, and these are displayed on the classroom wall. When someone uses his or her voice in a "violent" way, his or her badge is removed from the wall. This practice helps staff and students reduce the sarcasm and bullying that can all too readily be accepted as part of everyday life.

A local radio station has been very supportive of the campaign. Not only has it aired news stories, but has also recorded a sample of teachers, parents, bus drivers, and students taking the pledge. These recordings are played daily as public service announcements for the balance of the school year.

Fair and Safe Play (see page 70) and Bully Busters, which teaches long-term bully management strategies to teachers, students, and parents, are other programs followed at the school. The Voices campaign fits perfectly with both. If just one child has the newfound confidence to say: "Your voice hurt me—stop it," then the campaign has done its job.

THE CAMPAIGN PLEDGE

I pledge that I will not use my voice to hurt,

ridicule, belittle, or bully anyone.

If I ever forget this pledge, I promise to try,

try again until my voice is never

again used for violence.

John MacNeil Elementary School

62 Leaman Drive
Dartmouth, Nova Scotia
B3A 2K9 • 902-464-2488

Sunflower Garden Program

The Sunflower Garden Program was developed by teachers Neilena Corra and Debby White. The program recognizes children who perform good deeds and use kind language—both examples of positive behavior—in the classroom, on the school grounds, and within the community. The good deeds are recorded on "sunflowers"—made with bright yellow construction paper—and displayed in the main hallways of the school. The program has had a profound impact on the overall school environment.

The sunflower was chosen for the following reasons:

- It represents strength and confidence.

- It is highly visible.

- It stands erect and proud.

- It aims high with its head held toward the sun.

- Its colors represent all races.

- It represents the sun's warmth and growth.

- Its seeds are plentiful and strong.

On the playground, "Sun Catchers" (students in grades five and six) are watchful observers who record positive behaviors in the Sunflower Garden Book. The "Sun Catchers" are easy to recognize in their bright yellow hats.

The community is also encouraged to contact the school to tell of good deeds observed within the community.

An important aspect of this program involves monthly themes. Each grade level is assigned a month, and each month one grade's artwork is displayed on the Giving Tree, a white birch that stands in the school foyer. Here is a sample of monthly themes:

October: Junior elementary classes were matched with senior classes to make sunflowers out of beads. Photos of the students were glued in the centers of these flowers.

November: Mirror shapes reflected students' thoughts about friendship.

February: Heart bracelets were made by the students and worn on Valentine's Day. These bracelets promoted a discussion on love of friends and family. Students were encouraged to use the opening statement, "I love it when..." and to end the statement with a positive thought. After Valentine's Day, the bracelets were hung on the tree for the remainder of the month.

March: The focus was on Wisdom Pouches. These are small bags made of green cotton and tied with ribbons. Inside each pouch, teachers placed a typewritten passage that contained words of wisdom. The pouches were hung on the Giving Tree. At the beginning of each morning and afternoon session, a student selected a pouch and read the message found inside over the P.A. system.

April: Ribbon awards indicated ways in which students could help "Mother Earth." On Earth Day (April 22), students gathered in the foyer and read their messages to other classes.

May: Baskets, containing promises for carrying out good deeds for mothers, were hung on the Giving Tree.

June: This was seed-planting month. All students were given milk cartons in which to plant their sunflower seeds. As well, seeds were planted around the school. In September, giant sunflowers greeted the children when they returned to school.

Kingston Elementary School

Box 295
Kingston, Nova Scotia
B0P 1R0 • 902-765-7530

Kingston Elementary School has been a Comprehensive Guidance and Counseling Program pilot and implementation site since August 1996. This program espouses a provincial framework, which includes an advisory committee, needs assessments, resource identification and allocation, activity design and implementation, learner and program outcomes, and evaluation. The program is comprised of four domains (personal, social, education, and career) and four components (guidance curriculum; counseling, consultation, coordination; life/career planning; program management and system support). The program actively involves staff, students, and parents. It is both preventative/proactive and responsive/reactive in nature.

The program equips students with the attitudes and competencies they need to function as lifelong learners, critical thinkers, effective problem solvers and decision makers, and productive and fulfilled citizens.

The following are some initiatives undertaken by the school.[2]

- Anger Response Inventory

  Assisted a local psychologist in establishing norms at the grades 4-7 level for this measure of temper control.

- Blue Thunder

  The police band presented a concert to local schools with a focus on staying drug-free.

- Child and Adolescent Services

  Positive Parenting sessions offered on topics of self-esteem, discipline, divorce, sibling rivalry, friends, anger management, and depression.

- Classroom Sessions

  Presentations offered on anger management, respect, assertiveness, divorce, bullying, friendship, diversity, stealing, and boy-girl relationships.

- Diversity In-Service

  Diversity workshops for students (see pages 40-41).

---

2. Beth Robinson, guidance counselor, kindly summarized the list.

- Drug-Awareness Poster Contests

  Lions Club contests.

  Knights of Columbus contests for grades 3-7.

- Family Resource Centre

  Entire school participated in United Nations projects such as making posters and writing essays.

  Invitation came from Greenwood Family Resource Centre (local military base) whose staff wanted to recognize our peacekeepers serving overseas.

- Grade-Three Parent Discussion Groups

  Parents of grade-three students were invited to discuss the influence of media on violence, children and stress, themes of violence in kids' reading and writing.

- Home and School

  Sessions held on drug education, common-sense parenting, bullying.

- Lending Library

  Guidance library with literature for students, parents, and staff; videos, audiotapes, and classroom kits on a variety of topics including bullying, anti-violence, assertiveness, respect, diversity, friendship, and peace education.

- Lions Club International Peace Poster Contest

  New theme each year ("A New Beginning for Peace" was the theme one year).

- Mediation Presentations

  School counselor co-presented at League of Peaceful Schools conference and Nova Scotia School Boards Association conference on topic of peer mediation in the elementary setting.

- Mediation Training

  One-day off-site training conferences held for aspiring mediators from local schools.

- Mediation Video

  Five grade-seven peer mediators performed a mediation play, which included raps, chants, explanation of mediation, and two demonstrations of mediation. The play was taped to use in future training and education sessions.

- Newsletter Entries

  Monthly entries on topics such as nonviolent crisis intervention, Tourette's syndrome, bullying, helping children deal with death, mediation.

- Nonviolent Crisis Intervention Training

  Staff from local schools received training.

- Panel Presentation for Staff

  Presenters included representatives from the R.C.M.P., Family and Children's Services, and Valley Youth Alternatives who engaged staff in discussion on issues of neglect, abuse, assault, and illegal activities as they relate to students and their families.

- Parent Education for Separating and Divorcing Parents

  School counselor participated in court-recommended sessions for parents offered by Kentville Justice Department.

  Incorporated learning about "I" messages (see page 42); impact of separation and divorce on children at different stages of development

- Parent Sessions

  Sunburst videos titled *Good Discipline, Good Kids, Keeping Peace at Home,* and *Helping Your Child Succeed at School* used as springboards for discussion.

- Patterns of Anger Response Questionnaire (PARQ)

  Designed by school counselor to help children in elementary school reflect on and become more attuned to their anger experiences.

  Explored physical, cognitive, and behavioral responses as well as productive approaches to resolving conflict.

- Peace Cranes

  With assistance from a Japanese visitor who trained older students to help younger students, we created two mobiles in Canada's official colors: red and white.

- Peace Plaques and Banners

  Displayed outside classrooms to denote success in achieving/maintaining peaceful classroom climate.

- Peaceful School In-Service

  Staff attended an in-service that focused on peaceful initiatives. We articulated our vision of a peaceful school and identified what we had accomplished and what remained to be accomplished. Later, we held a Celebration of Peace in-service for all students.

- Peace Tables

  Established in classrooms for negotiation and mediation.

  Some have peace fairy, peace bear, and so on as mascot.

  Official openings presided over by peer mediators with a "ribbon" cutting.

- A Peal for Peace

  Bell theme carried throughout school (League of Peaceful Schools initiative) (see page 39).

- Postcards for Veterans

  Grade-six students sent Remembrance Day postcards to war veterans.

- Promotion of Mediation

  Peer mediators read stories and put on skits and demonstrations in assemblies and classrooms (see pages 59-61).

  Mediators officially "opened" peace tables in classrooms, complete with "ribbon" cutting.

  Peer mediators participated in a mediation video.

  Article on mediation sent home in school newsletter.

- Racing Against Drugs

  R.C.M.P. taught students about healthy choices in the areas of drugs, wilderness survival, youth and the law, safety around electricity.

- RCH Staff In-Services

  In-services offered by the district RCH[3] coordinator encouraging celebration of diversity.

- Restorative Justice (Community Justice Forum) (see page 44-45)

  School counselor trained with R.C.M.P.

  Crisis response team introduced to the process and its applicability to the school setting.

---

3. RCH refers to: Race Relations-Cross Cultural Understanding-Human Rights.

- School In-Services

  Peter Davison, Family Violence Prevention Initiative; influence of media; emotional intelligence; Second Step.®

- School Spirit Assembly

  Students asked to come up with a song, rap, or chant about why they are glad to be part of Kingston Elementary School.

- Second Step® Program

  A violence prevention program used as a school-wide violence prevention curriculum for grades P-7.[4]

  A Family Guide to Second Step® offered as six-session parent complement.

- Stress Management In-Service

  Two day in-service that looked at sources, symptoms, and solutions held for staff at end of school year.

  In-service looked at managing stress in the face of turmoil in the education system and included a component of humor.

- Town Hall

  Grade six and seven classes introduced to democratic process as they engaged in debate and discussion on contentious issues.

Monthly Themes

A theme is assigned to each month. For example, the theme for September is Respect. The following activities reflect the school's commitment to promoting respect by all for all:

- Whole-school assembly during Peace Week with each class demonstrating a peace or respect chant.

- All students wear white shirts to represent unity, peace.

- All staff and students make a handprint in paint, affix name, and display along inner school walls in a rainbow of colors.

- Each class writes a pledge for peace or respect—to be displayed in the hallway outside of the classroom (stays up for the year).

- Display case filled with items representing diversity/acceptance/respect.

- Good News Awards bulletin board.

---

4. The Second Step® program is available from: Committee for Children, 568 First Ave. South, Suite 600, Seattle, WA 98104-2804.

- Students invited to submit essays and/or drawings that explore the theme of respect.

- Communicate with home through a "What's Happening" column in the school newsletter.

- Dedicate a peace flag.

- Create a "Respect" banner to be displayed in the library.

●●●●●

I presented the League of Peaceful Schools' flag to Kingston Elementary School at an assembly. After the presentation, I was moved by the reading of the following two poems—one was written by the principal, Jane Baskwill, and the other was written by Teri Sproule, a former student.

IF PEACE IS

If peace is a candle,
I'll light it each night.

If peace is a hand,
I'll hold on so tight.

If peace is a book,
I'll read it again.

If peace is a game,
I'll stay till the end.

If peace is a bell,
I'll make it ring.

If peace is a song,
I'll want to sing.

But peace is more than all of these things.
More than a book or a bell that rings.

Peace is a promise,
A pledge that we make
To help and protect,
For each other's sake.

If peace is a promise,
Then it's something we do.
For peace is a promise
Kept always by you!

—Jane Baskwill, principal

MY WORLD

In my world,
There is no color.
No difference between black and white.
And all people, animals, and all other living things
Are treated equally.

In my world,
There is no violence.
No reason for prejudice and war.
And all people, animals, and all other living things
Are treated with respect.

In my world,
There is no crime.
No reason for burglary and bankruptcy.
And all people, animals, and all other living things
Are treated with kindness.

In my world,
There is no abuse.
No reason for hitting and pain.
And all people, animals, and all other living things
Are greeted with happiness.

This could be our world someday
If we tried.

— Teri Sproule, former student

A PEAL FOR PEACE

In 1981, the United Nations General Assembly declared the third Tuesday of September be officially observed as International Day of Peace.

People across Canada, the delegates of the United Nations Assembly, and others in more than 50 countries around the world share a moment of silent contemplation on the day to reaffirm their commitment to world peace. Following the minute of silence, bells peal to celebrate hope for world peace.

A Peal for Peace provides us with a global ritual. It enables millions of us to proclaim, at the same time, our hope for world peace. We all share a desire to preserve the planet and everything that lives on it. When we celebrate A Peal for Peace, we acknowledge our common humanity—despite the diverse interests and beliefs of the human family.

Here are some ideas for promoting A Peal for Peace:

- Write a visual messages of peace on the playground.
- Ring the school bell.
- Make origami peace cranes.
- Link arms to form a peace chain.
- Write peace messages, and form them into a chain.
- Raise the flag of the United Nations.
- Organize a march for peace.
- Create an "A Peal for Peace" banner.
- Create a "World of People" map.

At an assembly (or in a classroom), play or sing one or more of the following songs:

- We Are the World
- From a Distance
- Peace Is Flowing Like a River
- I'd Like to Teach the World to Sing
- Imagine

DIVERSITY WORKSHOP

Read the following story to students:

Welcome to the year 2036. You awaken to the hum of your alarm clock, which is the same model preprogrammed to go off at the same time in every household in your neighborhood every day. Sleepily, you shuffle to your feet, and then begin the exercise regime that every mother, father, and child is doing beside his or her bed at this very moment. Twenty stretches, twenty push-ups, twenty sit-ups, twenty more stretches, twenty jumping jacks—you know the routine by heart. Fully awake now, you enter the shower, which is preset at the same temperature in every house and runs for five minutes before shutting off.

It doesn't really matter which house you wake up in—each has exactly the same floor plan. Each home has three bedrooms, a galley kitchen, bathroom, and technology room. Each house is a beige semi-detached structure with three trees planted on the front lawn and two in the backyard. A charcoal-gray Commuter, the only color and model of car manufactured now, sits in the paved driveway. All household furnishings are the same style and color; they are easy to replace should something wear out.

After your shower, you slip into your black and gray one-piece work uniform. Everyone wears the same uniform regardless of his or her assigned job. While different jobs are available, they are mainly in construction and manufacturing. The choices are not what they were in the 1900s. For example, it is no longer necessary to raise farm animals or crops. All meals and snacks come in a vitamin capsule, which provides all the necessary nutrients and calories. You swallow a Meal-Tab with water, five times a day. The Meal-Tab saves everyone hours each day—meal preparation and clean-up are things of the past, and the need for dining rooms in houses, cafeterias in schools, and lunch rooms in the workplace is eliminated.

You are assigned homes in neighborhoods where everyone works at the same plant or in the same office. In this way, cars are pooled so that you only have to drive your car every second day, sharing with the couple that lives in the other half of your house. You don't need to run errands since shopping is done over the home computer.

Children are no longer involved in extracurricular activities such as sports and music. Kids are bused to schools where each grade works at individual computer workstations in a large room from 8:30 a.m.-4:30 p.m. At each grade level, all students do the same work at the same time at their computer station. Everyone graduates from school at the age of 22. At home and at school, kids listen to music and play virtual sports on their personal computers during spare time. They wear navy school uniforms and shoes, making it easy to know what to put on in the morning. Kids and adults all wear the same hairstyle—cut at chin length and parted in the middle.

One noticeable change that has taken place over the years: all girls have black hair and all boys have medium brown hair. However, everyone has the same blue-gray eyes and light brown complexion. No one wears glasses because nobody has vision problems anymore. Nor is there a need for braces, hearing aids, or wheelchairs. Medical technology has eliminated most health problems. Consequently, the normal life span is 98 years, at which time the heart tends to give out. Men and women remain in the work force until this time.

The work week runs from Monday through Saturday, with three fifteen-minute nutrition breaks each day. One week of holidays is granted twice a year, but nobody goes away. People use their computers and virtual reality technology to visit ski hills in Switzerland and the warm waters of the Caribbean. They visit friends and family via e-mail and the "optiview" telephone system.

Families never have to move to a new home because everyone stays at the same job for life. Since adults live in the same neighborhood as their coworkers, young men and women marry someone from the same occupation they have been assigned to. A mother or father is permitted to stay home with a new baby until the infant reaches his or her first birthday. At that time, the toddler enters a daycare at the parents' place of employment. The child remains there until the age of four, when public schooling begins. Each family is allowed two children.

No one has live pets—computers provide virtual pets that offer the fun of pet ownership without the work. Each person in the family has his or her own computer in the technology room (called the living room until 2025). The computers are equipped with the same assortment of games, videos, and music in each home. Because kids are engaged in the same learning and leisure activities each day, there really isn't much for classmates or siblings to disagree about. Nor is there any arguing with parents over clothes or food.

In 2036, daily patterns, routines, and lifestyles are stable and predictable. Life is quite peaceful, even if it lacks the excitement and change of the old days.

•••••

Ask the following questions to initiate a discussion:

■ What do you think about this view of the future?

■ Would you like to live this lifestyle?

■ What do you like about it?

■ What do you not like about it?

Following the discussion, ask students:

■ What does *diversity* mean?

■ In what ways are people different?

■ What is good about being different from each other?

■ What is not so good about being different from each other?

■ Is it okay to be different?

■ What does *prejudice* mean?

■ What does *tolerance* mean?

■ What does *acceptance* mean?

■ What does *celebration* mean?

"I" MESSAGES

"I" messages are used to convey the impact of another's behavior or actions on us, without putting the other person on the defensive by using the accusatory "you." It is important to remember that no one can make us angry, sad, furious, or hurt. We each choose how to perceive and respond to a situation. Therefore, we need to take ownership of our own feelings.

Avoid statements such as:

■ *You make* me so angry!

■ *You make* me extremely frustrated!

■ *Your* insensitivity *makes* me want to cry!

■ *Your* selfishness *hurts* me deeply.

The message is more likely to have the desired result if all-inclusive terms are avoided:

■ *You never* arrive on time.

■ *You always* do this to me.

■ You are the *worst* procrastinator.

■ You are the *biggest* cheapskate!

It also helps to remain focused on the present, and avoid dredging up old issues:

■ Here we go again.

■ It's the same old story.

■ This is just like the last time.

■ When are you ever going to change?

The formula for an "I" message is simple:

■ *I feel* (name the emotion)

■ *when* (describe the situation, what happened)

■ *because* (how it affected you)

■ *and I want/need* (what you would like to see happen)

Focusing on our feelings and needs is more effective in garnering the other person's understanding and support than using negative approaches such as blaming, accusing, name-calling, insults, and sarcasm. Encourage students to put themselves in the other person's shoes and imagine how they might react with each approach. Their feelings and reactions to a situation may be quite valid. However, if the goal is to solve the problem, the "I" message is solution-oriented and, therefore, more likely to succeed.

RESTORATIVE JUSTICE

Background

Restorative justice is a way of thinking about crime and conflict that challenges us to re-examine traditional punitive responses to crime. Restorative justice models focus on holding offenders accountable in a meaningful way, repairing the harm done, and reintegrating the offender into the community.

Rationale for Restorative Justice

- Acknowledges direct and indirect victims
- Victim satisfaction
- Justice best determined by those directly affected
- Greater compliance when agreement drafted in company of community of care

Legal System

- Retributive justice
- Condemns offender
- Stigmatization
- Reactive

Community Justice Forum

- Restorative justice
- Condemns behavior
- Reintegrative shaming
- Proactive, preventative

Traditional Approach to Dealing With Offenses

- Reactive as opposed to preventative, proactive
- Adversarial
- Confrontational
- Investigative
- Objective
- Impersonal
- Focuses on offender
- Victim may feel neglected
- Focuses on correction, deterrence, punishment, restitution, revenge; little emphasis on empathy, rehabilitation, reparation, mending relationship; primary objective is protection of public
- Rate of re-offending a concern

Ideal Intervention

- Proactive, preventative
- Rehabilitative
- Victim support
- Victim involvement
- Empathy, remorse
- No recidivism
- Restitution and reparation—symbolic and material
- Respect for persons, property, societal norms, and laws

COMMUNITY JUSTICE FORUM

Facilitator Script

Welcome everyone. My name is _____, and I will be facilitating the community justice forum that you have all agreed to participate in today. Before we begin, I'd like to introduce each participant and indicate his or her reason for being here. (Introductions; explanation of relationship to victim or offender, co-facilitator)

Thanks to each of you for being willing to take part in a community justice forum. It is likely that each of you is feeling somewhat uncomfortable and anxious about what will take place. I hope this brief outline of the purpose and procedure will address some of the concerns you might have.

The goal of a community justice forum is to deal with the inappropriate or unacceptable actions of an individual by engaging in a problem-solving procedure that attacks the problem, not the person. Community justice forums share some of the characteristics of mediation. Through the forum, we explore how each person has been affected by the choices of the offender, and we seek approaches to restorative justice to repair the harm that has been done. Each person here has a part to play and contributes to the final outcome.

The incident we are here to discuss is _____ that took place on _____. _____ has admitted his/her part in the incident and has agreed to address the impact in a community justice forum. However, if at any time _____ no longer wishes to participate, he/she may leave. The matter then will be dealt with through another avenue.

If agreement is reached in this forum, and _____ satisfactorily carries out the terms of the agreement, then this matter will be considered to have been dealt with and will proceed no further.

Exploration of Impact

To the offender (if more than one, have each speak in turn):

- Please tell us what happened by summarizing the incident for us.

- How did you come to be involved?

- What were you thinking about at the time?

- What have you thought about since?

- Who do you think has been affected by your actions?

- In what way have they been affected?

To the victim (if more than one, have each respond in turn):

- Do you have anything to add to the summary of what happened?

- What did you think at the time?

- What did you think later?

- What was the worst part?

- How has this incident affected you?

- How has this incident affected your friends and family?

To the victim's supporters:

- How did you find out about the incident?

- What did you think when you first heard about it?

- How has it affected you?

To the offender's supporters:

- It must be very difficult for you to hear this.

- How did you find out about the incident?

- What did you think when you first heard about the incident?

- How has it affected you?

To the offender:

- Is there anything else you want to say to _____ or to anyone else?

Reparation

To the victim:

- You've had a chance to share your thoughts and feelings and to hear from all of the parties. What would you like to see happen as a result of this forum?

To the victim's supporters:

- What suggestions do you have for repairing the harm that's been done?

To the offender:

- Do you think that what is being asked of you is fair?

- Do you have any suggestions?

To the offender's supporters:

- Do you feel comfortable with the proposed agreement for restitution and reparation?

- Do you have any suggestions to offer?

To all participants:

We will need to designate a person or persons to monitor the carrying out of the agreement and to ensure that all aspects have been completed satisfactorily.

I will read the agreement to you to make sure I have included all the key elements and necessary details, such as a time line. Before you leave, I'll ask that each of you sign the agreement, and I will make a photocopy for each of you.

I feel that we made significant progress today in beginning to address some of the hurt, anger, disgust, shock, embarrassment, humiliation, distrust, resentment, and/or fear that some of you may have been feeling when you first arrived. _____'s completion of this agreement will contribute to the healing process for all involved.

Thank you for your involvement in this community justice forum.

(Make copies, and hand out the final agreement. Encourage some informal talk after the session— it is during this time when much of the integration is likely to occur.)

Annapolis East Elementary School

PO Box 640
Middleton, Nova Scotia
B0S 1P0 • 902-825-5330

Peace Week

Annapolis East began its commitment to building a culture of peace under the leadership of principal Heather Harris. To assess progress, all violent incidents in the school are tracked through incident forms. Interestingly, after tracking behavior for two years, the school chose the week of May 22 for Peace Week—for both years, it had been the week with the highest number of incidents. A great strategy!

Peace Week ends with a school-wide assembly. One year, the theme of the assembly was Turning Bullies Into Buddies. Throughout the day, six groups presented what they had done and learned.

Some of the presentations included:

■ **Wash Away the Bully Blues** (grade three)

Two students held a clothesline while the other students pinned shirts (made from construction paper) on the clothesline. Each shirt had ideas on it for ways to respond to being bullied. For example:

- Report the Problem
- Ask for Help
- Stay in Control
- Stick with Friends
- Make Wise Choices
- Don't Insult
- Invite Them to Play

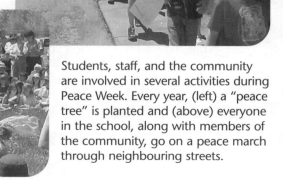

Students, staff, and the community are involved in several activities during Peace Week. Every year, (left) a "peace tree" is planted and (above) everyone in the school, along with members of the community, go on a peace march through neighbouring streets.

During Peace Week, all classes decorate their doors. This design was on the door of a grade 4/5 classroom.

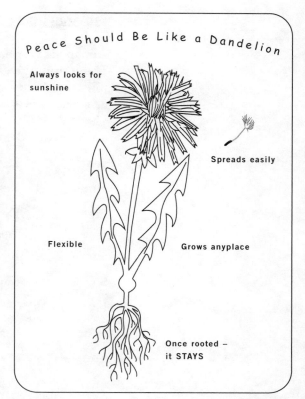

- **Peace Walk of Chalk** (school-wide)

  All students in the school wrote peaceful messages on the sidewalk with chalk.

- **Origami** (grade four)

  Students folded origami animals and created messages such as:

  - "Roaring for peace" (lion)

  - "Stick your neck out for peace" (giraffe)

  - "Batty over peace" (bat)

- **Peaceful Doorways** (school-wide)

  All the classroom doors were decorated, in keeping with the school theme.

- **Peace Person**

  On mural paper, students drew and colored life-sized people. They labeled their people as follows:

  - Head: "Positive mental attitude to have peaceful thoughts that will result in peaceful action."

  - Eyes: "To see the good in everyone."

  - Ears: "To hear and sympathize with others."

  - Neck: "To stick out for others when they are in trouble."

  - Hands: "For helping and sharing."

  - Legs: "To walk the extra mile for others."

  - Feet: "To share your peace and joy with friends."

One student's "peace person."

Ten-Step Plan

Annapolis East has both a student and a staff Peaceful School Committee. These committees are responsible for introducing new ideas and initiatives. The committees also keep on top of the progress and achievements of students, teachers, and parents as they follow the ten-step plan. In addition, the School Advisory Council and community members are invited and encouraged to contribute to keep the plan active.

Ten	Develop Partnerships
Nine	Respect and Protect[5]
Eight	Develop Creative and Effective Consequences and Alternatives
Seven	Revise Discipline Policy
Six	Support the Partners with Resources
Five	Training for Peer Mediators
Four	Classroom Curriculum—Peaceful School
Three	Positive School Morale
Two	Peaceful School Week
One	Peace Flag
Zero	Commitment to No Tolerance for Violence

---

5. *Respect & Protect* by Carole Remboldt and Richard N. Zimman.

Peaceful Alphabet

This alphabet was written by students in an upper elementary class.

A	Be Attentive not Angry
B	Be a Buddy not a Bully
C	Be Caring not Cranky
D	Be a Dear not Demanding
E	Be Expressive not Explosive
F	Be Friendly don't Fight
G	Be Good not Greedy
H	Be Helpful not Hurtful
I	Be Inspirational not Ignorant
J	Be Joyous not Jealous
K	Be Kind don't Kid
L	Be Lovable not Low
M	Be Merry not Mean
N	Be Nice not Naughty
O	Be Open-Minded not Offensive
P	Be Peaceful not Picky
Q	Be Quiet don't Quarrel
R	Be Respectful not Rude
S	Be Sweet not Sour
T	Be Truthful not Trouble
U	Be Understanding not Unkind
V	Be Valuable not Vicious
W	Be Warm not Wicked
X	Be open to Xs and Os and don't expect everything to go your way
Y	Be Yielding don't Yell
Z	Be Zealous don't act Zany

R. B. Dickey Elementary School

14 Dickey Street
Amherst, Nova Scotia
B4H 2H9 • 902-661-2460

Several school-wide initiatives, developed by Robert Angel, former principal of R. B. Dickey, contribute to a climate that encourages students to be caring, responsible citizens.

C.R.E.A.T.E.

C.R.E.A.T.E. (Cultural Recreational Activity Time in Education) is an activity-based enrichment program intended to extend, broaden, and deepen children's educational experiences. Each Friday afternoon for eight weeks, all students from grades three to six are involved in enrichment programs. From a list of as many as eighteen programs, students select three or four in order of preference. Whenever possible, students are assigned to their first choice. The programs, instructed by teachers, parents, and community members, instill in students a sense of pride and responsibility and help build a positive spirit in the school. Programs operate both within the school and within the community. Since its inception several years ago, C.R.E.A.T.E. programs have included: Babysitting Basics, Ready…Set…Type, Learning to Draw, Making Videos, Tasty Treats, Ukelele, Fly Tying, Pencil Art, Creative Drama, Computer Basics, Water Safety and CPR, Guitar Instruction.

P.A.C.

Twenty-four grade-six students plan, organize, and coordinate eight different activities during recess each day. Dressed in bright red vests, P.A.C. (Program Activity Coordinators) members are easily recognized on the playground. P.A.C. members meet monthly to discuss new games and sort out inefficiencies in the activities. Since the P.A.C. team was introduced, playground conflict has been reduced by 80 percent!

C.A.R.E.S.

Under the C.A.R.E.S. (Children At Risk Experiencing Success) program, a designated teacher is available one morning per week to meet with students who require either academic support or support with life/social skills. The C.A.R.E.S. teacher works with students, parents, community support personnel, and other teachers to develop a strategy for the students under his or her care. A school psychologist is available to assist the C.A.R.E.S. teachers with serious counseling situations and to conduct workshops.

Tell me—I'll forget.
Show me—I'll understand.
Involve me—I'll remember.

—Chinese proverb

Sambro Elementary School

3725 Old Sambro Road
Sambro, Nova Scotia
B3V 1G1 • 902-868-2717

At Sambro Elementary, the walls reflect the school's commitment to a safe and positive learning environment. Children's artwork, posters, and motivational thoughts are all on display.

Thought for the Week

Each week, a "thought for the week" is posted for students and staff to reflect upon. These thoughts are adapted from *The Family Virtues Guide*.[6]

Some examples are:

- I am assertive. I think for myself and do what is right. I tell the truth about what is just. I have the right to be treated with respect.

- I care for others and myself. I pay loving attention to people and things I care about. I give my best to each job.

- I have compassion. I notice when someone needs attention and freely offer my help.

- I am considerate of others. I think about how my actions affect them. I think of thoughtful things that bring happiness to others.

- I have the courage to try new things. I admit my mistakes and learn from them. I listen with my heart. I have the courage to do what is right.

- I am courteous. I remember my manners and treat people with respect. I greet others politely. I show people that I care.

- I am forgiving of myself and others. I learn from my mistakes. I have the power to keep changing for the better.

- I am gentle. I speak and act with gentleness. I show care for people and for everything I touch.

- I am helpful. I look for ways in which I can be of service. I care for others and myself. I look for ways to make a difference.

- I am honest. I have integrity. I tell the truth, kindly and tactfully. I have no need to impress others or follow the crowd. I do what I know is right.

---

6. *The Family Virtues Guide* by Linda Kavelin Popov.

A peace display at a local mall. In Nova Scotia, biannually, a select number of school districts are invited to display student work in the local shopping malls. This initiative, organized by the Nova Scotia Teachers Union, is called "Schools Today."

Peer Mediation

If you set the right example, you won't need to worry about the rules.

—Anonymous

Peer mediation plays a very important role in the school's proactive approach to discipline. The following excerpt from Sambro Elementary School's Code of Behavior reflects this approach.

> In our view, discipline focuses on problem prevention, the development of self-control and consequences based on mutual respect and social responsibility.

> In this Code of Behavior we have attempted to reflect the positive school climate that the school wishes to embody in all its functions and activities.

In addition to resolving disputes, the peer mediators facilitate classroom workshops throughout the school year (see pages 59-61).

During one of my visits to the school, the peer mediators organized and facilitated a school-wide assembly in which each class was offered an opportunity to showcase the lessons they had learned in the workshops conducted by the mediators.

The highlight of the assembly was "Who Wants to be a Peacekeeper?, " Sambro's rendition of the television game show, *Who Wants to Be a Millionaire?* The peer mediators wrote and directed this entertaining and insightful version. Game participants were volunteers from the audience (see pages 53-58).

WHO WANTS TO BE A PEACEKEEPER? [7]

Instructions (everyone in the class is invited to participate):

1. Signal/raise your hand if you know the answer to the question.

2. The first person to raise his or her hand attempts to answer the question.

3. The first six students to answer correctly continue to the next round, followed by the next four, then two, then, finally, one.

4. Everyone who participates receives a certificate; the winner of each round wins a first-place, second-place, third-place, or fourth-place certificate.

You are in the washroom, and two of your classmates walk in and start writing on the walls. You...

A. Stay out of sight, and don't let them know you've seen them.

B. Grab the pen away.

C. Join in.

D. Leave, and report the incident to the principal.

You are outside eating your recess snack, and your friend grabs your snack without asking. You...

A. Push her.

B. Tell her it's rude, and ask her to give it back.

C. Grab her recess snack.

D. Call her a name.

You are playing soccer, and someone accidentally kicks the ball at you. You...

A. Say it's okay but to please be more careful next time.

B. Kick the ball at him.

C. Make a fuss.

D. Tell him he can't play.

---

7. Developed at Sambro Elementary by the following students: Kayla Clarke, Heather Blom, Alexa Minichiello, Melissa MacDonald, Claire Piccinin, and Emily Flemming, under the guidance of Lee Paul.

Your team lost the game, and someone on the other team rubs it in. You...

A. Ask, "What's the problem?" and kick the ball at him.

B. Ask him to stop, and walk away.

C. Scream a rude name.

D. Complain to your friend.

You are in the principal's office because you weren't listening to your teacher. Someone walks by and makes fun of you. You...

A. Yell at her.

B. Poke your tongue out at her.

C. Ignore her, and keep from getting in more trouble.

D. Leave the office.

You see some students playing basketball, and you would like to join in the game. You...

A. Grab the ball without asking.

B. Brag about how good you are.

C. Ask if they need another player.

D. Say nothing, and hope they notice you.

One of your friends tells another friend something that was a secret between you and her. You...

A. Run away, and cry.

B. Tell a secret about her.

C. Explain to your friend that it was private, and ask her not to repeat it again.

D. Call her a name, and never speak to her again.

**You are at church, and a dime falls
from the collection plate. You...**

A. Pick it up, and put it back.

B. Kick it under the seat for later.

C. Put it in your pocket.

D. Pretend it was yours, and keep it.

**You see your friend steal candy
from a store. You...**

A. Tell the store clerk.

B. Keep it a secret.

C. Confront your friend, and tell him to put it back.

D. Eat the candy too.

**You are walking home from school, and
someone is following you. You...**

A. Tell him to get lost.

B. Take a shortcut through the park.

C. Go to the nearest safe house, and tell an adult.

D. Ignore him, and hope he goes away.

**You just got a new haircut, and some
people are making fun of it. You...**

A. Tell them you like it and that they are not being very nice.

B. Tell them their hair is ugly.

C. Pull their hair.

D. Run away, and cry.

You are on the monkey bars, and someone is pulling you off. You...

A.   Try to kick her.

B.   Yell at her.

C.   Jump off, and run away.

D.   Tell her it's dangerous to do that, and ask her to wait for her turn.

You are searching in your desk for a pencil, and you remember your friend has it. You...

A.   Ask for it back.

B.   Grab it from his hand.

C.   Run, and tell the teacher while she is teaching.

D.   Call him a thief.

You are in line for recess, and someone pushes in front of you. You...

A.   Get in front of him, and bump into other people.

B.   Politely ask him to go to the back of the line.

C.   Push him out of line.

D.   Yell at him.

Your friend has been deserting you lately and hanging out with someone else. You...

A.   Say mean things about him.

B.   Tell him in private how you feel.

C.   Give him the "cold shoulder," and ignore him.

D.   Sit around sulking and hope that he will notice.

You get in trouble for cheating but it was really your friend who cheated. You...

A. Tell her you are no longer friends.

B. Tell her it's not fair that you were blamed, and ask her to tell the teacher the truth.

C. Take the blame like a good friend.

D. Cheat next time because you will get blamed anyway.

Someone just made fun of you because you got a bad mark in math. You...

A. Say, "Oh well, I'll try to improve."

B. Tell him he's no good at math either.

C. Call him a name.

D. Complain to your mother.

Someone just pushed your friend in the mud on purpose. You...

A. Say, "You're a bully."

B. Tell her it was wrong, and ask what you can all do about it.

C. Push her in the mud.

D. Do nothing.

You just found the web site you were looking for, and someone comes along and pushes all the buttons causing you to lose the site. You...

A. Use an "I" message.

B. Yell at her.

C. Yell for the teacher.

D. Hit her.

Someone tells you your best friend has been gossiping about you. You...

A. Start gossiping about your friend.

B. Accuse your friend in front of the class.

C. Talk to her in private to see if it is true.

D. Trip her in gym class.

You just heard your friend make fun of a person from another culture. You...

A. Make fun too.

B. Tell him it is wrong, and you will not take part in it.

C. Say nothing at all.

D. Tell your sister about it later.

You and six friends go shopping at the mall. They steal socks and wait for you to steal too. You...

A. Tell the manager because you don't want to be accused.

B. What the heck, jump in too.

C. Let them get away with it. A few pairs of socks won't matter.

D. Brag about all the socks you already have.

You finish your math test. Your classmates ask you for the answer to the last question. You...

A. Tell them the answer.

B. Make a big scene.

C. Tell them to try it themselves.

D. Slip them the answer on a piece of paper.

A Workshop for Lower Elementary Students

Mediation is a vital part of the "curriculum of life" at Sambro. It is important, therefore, that all students have a good understanding of how the process works and when it is appropriate to call upon the mediators for assistance in resolving disputes. Peer mediators present the following role-play to students in grades P-1 to introduce them to the principles of mediation.

Instructions

To begin, the mediators facilitating this workshop give a brief introduction. They talk about how people handle conflicts differently and that conflicts can be resolved peacefully. They emphasize that it's okay to ask for help to find solutions—this is where mediators can assist.

The facilitators then explain that they are going to read a story called "The Muddy Mishap" (page 60) to help students understand how the mediation process works. The facilitators ask for some students to role-play the characters in the story.

The storyteller (one of the facilitators) starts the story while the characters follow the script and add simple actions. At about the halfway point in the story, the storyteller stops reading and a discussion is initiated (page 61). Following the discussion, the rest of the story is read and role-played.

A Summary of the Mediation Process

Ground Rules

- no interrupting
- no name-calling or put-downs
- agree to tell the truth
- agree to try hard to solve the problem

Steps in the Process

Telling the story:

- Disputant #1 tells what happened.
- Mediators summarize what was said.
- Disputant #1 explains how he or she feels about what happened and why.
- Mediators summarize the feelings.
- Disputant #2 tells what happened.
- Mediators summarize what was said.
- Disputant #2 explains how he or she feels about what happened and why.
- Mediators summarize the feelings.

Finding solutions:

- Disputant #1 is asked what he or she can do to solve the problem.
- Disputant #2 is asked what he or she can do to solve the problem.
- Get agreement to a solution from both disputants.
- Ask disputant #1 what he or she would do differently if this problem happened again.
- Ask disputant #2 what he or she would do differently if this problem happened again.
- Congratulate the disputants for solving their problem.

Role-Play: The Muddy Mishap

Characters:

Students in conflict: Alexa and Kory
Mediators: Veronica and Abdul
Teacher on duty

As the storyteller reads the story, the characters follow the script and add simple actions.

Storyteller:

The recess bell rang. Alexa quickly tied her sneakers and headed out the door toward the playground. The rain earlier that morning had left a few shallow puddles under the swings, but with a little care, Alexa knew she could avoid getting her feet too wet. "Great," thought Alexa, "an empty swing."

What Alexa didn't know was that Kory had just hopped off the swing to pick up his fallen recess snack. Alexa cleared the puddle and was about to sit on the seat. Kory did not see Alexa and, at that very same moment, made a grab for the swing. Alexa felt the sharp tug on the swing, but it was too late—down she went into the mud puddle. It was then that the teacher on duty turned to see a very muddy Alexa and a puzzled-looking Kory both holding the swing.

Start discussion (see page 61).

Role-Play continues...

Storyteller:

The teacher on duty asks Kory and Alexa, "What happened to you?" (They explain.) "I think this is something the mediators can help you with. Would you like to go to mediation?"

(The teacher finds Veronica and Abdul, the mediators, and introduces Kory and Alexa to them.) Kory and Alexa sit down with Veronica and Abdul, and they go through the ground rules and steps in the mediation process.

After Alexa and Kory understand the rules and process, they each tell what happened and how they feel. Following that, Veronica and Abdul ask them what they can do to solve their problem. When they agree on a solution, the mediators ask what they would do differently if something like this happened again.

To finish up, Kory and Alexa sign an agreement that says what they are going to do to solve the problem.

Remember: A peaceful solution is the best solution.

Discussion (led by workshop facilitators):

What do you think Alexa will do? (Remember she is covered with mud, and she thinks Kory grabbed the swing from her intentionally.) Do you think she will:

■ cry

■ push back

■ yell at Kory, and blame him for what happened

■ do nothing at all

■ walk away, and complain to her teacher after recess

■ tell her mother about it later

What do you think Kory will do? (Remember, all he expected was a turn on the swing.) Do you think he will:

■ jump on the swing

■ tell Alexa he was there first and she shouldn't have tried to take his swing away

■ apologize

Was the accident Alexa's fault or Kory's fault?

Do you think it will help if Alexa and Kory explain to each other what happened and how they feel? (Remember, they are both upset and worried they might be in trouble. They both think they have done nothing wrong, and they don't know how to solve their problem.)

Facilitators:

This is a situation where peer medication can help. If you have a problem or a conflict you cannot solve on your own, you should tell your teacher or another adult. He or she can help you find the mediators.

We would like to tell you a little more about mediation.

■ When you go to mediation, you are not "in trouble."

■ Deciding to talk to the mediators is a good decision.

■ Mediation is a peaceful way to solve a problem.

■ You will both have a chance to talk during mediation.

■ You will also have an opportunity to tell how you feel.

■ Mediators do not solve the problem for you. They just help you solve the problem.

■ Mediators do not punish you.

■ Mediators do not talk about the mediation with other students.

Go back to "The Muddy Mishap" on page 60.

Harrietsfield Elementary School

1150 Old Sambro Road
Harrietsfield, Nova Scotia
B3V 1B1 • 902-479-4230

Like the teachers at Sambro, Harrietsfield Elementary teachers consider the implications of peace in curriculum choices, in individual classes, and when developing school-wide programs. Principal Pam Nicholson-Comeau has been instrumental in establishing programs that help students learn to make good choices.

Effective Alternatives to Punishment

Students are actively involved in deciding appropriate consequences for their behavior, and the process is viewed as a learning opportunity. When dealing with inappropriate behavior, students are asked to write down the *Facts* (exactly what happened), the *Feelings* (their feelings as opposed to the feelings of others involved), and the *Future* (from what they have learned, what they would do differently if they ever again found themselves in a similar situation).

When appropriate, students are encouraged to write letters of apology to those involved, and include specific reference to the unacceptable behavior. For example, if a student writes an apology to someone for name-calling, he or she is encouraged to use kind, positive words to describe the person to whom the apology is intended.

P.A.L.S.

P.A.L.S. (Peaceful Action Leaves Smiles or, for the adults, Peace and Learning Strategies) is an intervention program that promotes peaceful and respectful behavior. Students, who are selected by teachers, explore and are encouraged to adopt appropriate and effective strategies for success in their relationships with others. They are also encouraged to explore their general feelings about themselves and their overall learning. All persons involved in this program are P.A.L.S. for one another and have P.A.L.S. throughout the school.

Students are accountable for their behavior, and their choices are discussed in a supportive environment with open, honest, and positive communication. In collaboration with teachers, administrators, and the students themselves, those in this program develop personal goals relating to peace and learning. They are exposed to a wide range of meaningful stories of positive changes that occur in people once the choices they make focus on peace and self-improvement. The stories also embrace multiculturalism and the importance of accepting individual differences.

The program involves participation in cooperative art projects that promote peace and teamwork. Students also take part in special events such as plays, movies, or dinners at nice restaurants.

In general, P.A.L.S. helps students increase self-esteem and, ultimately, personal success by offering them:

- opportunities for building friendships
- lessons in social skills
- strategies for peace and effective learning
- strategies for preventing violence and bullying
- opportunities for leadership roles

Christmas "Gifts"

During the Christmas season, students give a gift (of thankfulness) to someone or some group that has made a difference in their lives. These "gifts" are written on paper angels and displayed in the hallways.

Valentine's "Heart of Gold"

For Valentine's Day, teachers submit names of students "caught" in acts of kindness during the school year. Each student has his or her name displayed on a bulletin board in a paper heart. The names are also entered in a draw, and the winners of the draw each receive a book as a prize.

Town Hall

Like many other schools, Harrietsfield holds town hall meetings. During these assemblies, "Peace Angels" (designated students) look for cooperative students (and classes) who listen well and try to be the best they can be. These students are rewarded with various treats and awards after each assembly. Classes that have made improvements are also recognized.

Students constructed these paper quilt sections as part of an initiative promoting peace and teamwork.

Chebucto Heights Elementary School

230 Cowie Hill Road
Halifax, Nova Scotia
B3P 2M3 • 902-479-4298

Peace Takes Flight

"Peace Takes Flight, Our Wish for the New Millennium" was initiated as part of a special millennium project organized by the municipal government. Students made origami paper cranes (see pages 23-25)—an international symbol of peace—and sent them to friends and relatives in other parts of Canada and around the world. Each recipient was asked to send a postcard to the school telling about where he or she lives and to send the crane on to another

The permanent display of Peace Takes Flight

destination. Postcards were displayed and the "flights" of the cranes were tracked on a large map. At the conclusion of the project, a permanent display case was created highlighting the countries visited by the cranes. All of the postcards were complied into an album, which has become part of the school's library collection.

The Garden of Peace reflects the beauty of diversity. The garden, on display at a local mall, was part of the "Schools Today" initiative organized by the Nova Scotia Teachers Union.

Elmsdale District School

224 Highway 214
Elmsdale, Nova Scotia
B0N 1M0 • 902-883-5350

Primary Peacemaker Program

This program is based on the belief that every student is capable of
learning negotiation and mediation skills and benefits from the
opportunity to do so. Some of the conflict resolution initiatives developed
by primary teachers Faye Clark and Heather MacKeil include:

- Write a class book titled *120 Things to Do Instead of Hitting.*

- Rewrite the song "If You're Happy and You Know It" to "If You're
  Angry and You Know It."

- Create a traveling journal with class rules and class mascot to raise
  parent awareness about the peace program.

- **Pebbles for Peace:** When a positive behavior is observed, place a
  pebble in a jar. When the jar is full, hold a class celebration.

- **Pieces for Peace:** Scan a class photo, and cut it into puzzle pieces.
  When a positive behavior is observed, place a puzzle piece in a
  picture frame. When the puzzle is completed, a People for Peace
  celebration takes place.

- **Changing Places:** Standing in someone else's shoes helps one see things
  from the other side. To teach this step in the negotiation process, nail
  two pairs of shoes (facing each other) to a board. Students stand in one
  pair of shoes and are given an opportunity to speak. They then change
  places and tell how they understand what the other one feels. This is an
  essential negotiation skill.

- **Solution Station:** Place a peace mat in a corner of the classroom.
  Students are encouraged to go there to settle classroom disputes.
  While standing on the mat, each child involved in the conflict has an
  opportunity to tell his or her side of the story without interruption.
  Those involved in the dispute think of three solutions and choose the
  one they both agree with. (A student mediator of the day is available
  should they need help resolving their problem.) The following rules
  are reviewed and posted along with a list of "feeling words."

  - Tell the truth.

  - Talk one at a time.

  - No name-calling or put-downs.

- Find three ideas to solve the problem.

- Choose one idea you can agree on.

- Shake hands.

Students may then sign a peace chart and share their solution with you. This exercise helps students build their self-esteem and makes them more confident in their ability to resolve their own problems.

Home Extension: Have students make their own peace mats. On a carpet sample, they can design and paint a stencil, then use the mat to practice peacemaking skills at home.

Newsletter

Faye Clark and Heather MacKeil also produce a newsletter, *CHOOSE – IT…USE – IT.* In it, they share ideas (such as those mentioned above) with other interested educators.

Do what you can where you are with what you have.

—Anonymous

St. Joseph Elementary School

2 School Street
Sydney Mines, Nova Scotia
B1V 1R3 • 902-736-8382

At St. Joseph Elementary, students, staff, and community members work
year round to promote a peaceful learning environment. In addition to
daily activities, students and staff participate in several special events and
activities that focus on specific areas. Manners Matter Week and Peace
Week are two popular events. During both, teachers develop booklets
containing lesson plans and ideas to use in all classrooms. Parents are kept
informed of these initiatives through a newsletter. Parents are also
encouraged to attend assemblies and special events.

Manners Matter Week

During Manners Matter Week students are encouraged to:

- practice writing thank-you notes

- eat a meal together to practice table manners

- practice making introductions

- role-play using the telephone, taking messages, responding politely

Peace Week

During Peace Week, students are encouraged to participate in the
following activities:

- research people who have won the Nobel Peace Prize

- create a mascot for the school

- make a list of animals that represent peace, and explain why

- write about where they would go and with whom to find some
  "peace and quiet"

- use the peace pipe as an example of a symbol of peace, or write about
  another symbol of peace they might pass on to someone

- write a message of peace or a message that will cheer up someone. Put
  the messages in a box labeled "Pieces of Peace," and encourage anyone
  who needs his or her spirits lifted to take a message from the box, then
  replace it with a new one

- create TV commercials or newsbreaks that promote peace in the world

- read a message of peace every day over the P.A. system

East Richmond Education Centre

Box 219
St. Peter's, Nova Scotia
B0E 3B0 • 902-535-2029

There is a family feeling at East Richmond that has been created through a common vision of peace and through related activities and projects that support that vision. The school motto is "Together We Can Make a Difference."

Peace education is the heart of East Richmond. Every week, students and staff meet together in multi-age groups for peace lessons based on the themes of cooperation, positive emotional expression, acceptance, communication, and conflict resolution. A committee comprised of several staff members meets on a regular basis to plan these lessons. The lessons have been compiled into a book that continues to evolve and grow each year.

At East Richmond, evidence of the school's commitment to peace is everywhere. Visitors to the school immediately see that creating a culture of peace is one of the school's main goals—from the displays in the halls to decorated doors to a mural on the back wall of the stage. Many community members, parents, and local officials attend school-based events to celebrate the school's accomplishments in making it a place where peaceful living is enjoyed by all.

Community Outreach

East Richmond has developed a relationship with the residents of the local nursing care facility for the elderly. The students visit throughout the year and find ways of celebrating holidays and special events with the residents; for example, holding an Easter bonnet parade, delivering Valentine's Day cards, performing a Christmas concert and singing carols.

Students also make decorations at Christmas for local merchants. They then deliver cookies to the merchants and to those at the nursing care facility on "Cookie Day."

This peace assembly was attended by members of the community. Notice the "Peace is in Our Hands" mural located on the back wall of the stage. The year this mural was painted, every student in the school contributed a handprint—to symbolize his or her commitment to peace.

This tree is located in the school foyer. Throughout the year, the tree is decorated according to theme and/or season. This particular display was during Peace Week.

Bible Hill Central Elementary School

103 Pictou Road
Truro, Nova Scotia
B2N 2S2 • 902-896-5507

Fair and Safe Play

The Fair and Safe Play Program (Nova Scotia Sports and Recreation Commission) encourages fair and safe play in all areas of sports and recreation. The program also provides guidance, education, access to resources, and a solid foundation on which to build initiatives that are tailored to a community, a team, or any other group.

As a concept, Fair and Safe Play helps everyone increase his or her enjoyment of sport and recreational activities. The program is proactive and based on four main components:

- Fair Play Facilities
- Risk Management
- Education
- Awards

Play Fair Day

Bible Hill Elementary is one of the forerunners in adapting the Fair and Safe Play principles to the school environment. After a presentation at an in-service, the staff decided the program might alleviate an increasing concern about aggressive student interactions. The school recognized that success depended upon a solid understanding of the Fair Play goals by students, staff, and parents. As a result, Fair Play Day is held for the entire school community. The day includes workstations, a presentation on resolving conflict by a local theatre group, remarks by school staff and representatives from Sport and Recreation, the declaration of a "Fair Play Oath" (see page 71), and a basketball game.

The Bible Hill Fair Play principles are:

- Respect school rules.
- Respect the staff.
- Respect your peers.
- Give everyone an equal chance to participate.
- Maintain your self-control at all times.
- Be responsible for your actions.

FAIR PLAY OATH

We, the stakeholders of Fair Play at Bible Hill Central, promise on
this day to respect and follow the following principles of Fair Play
as set out in our Charter.

We have the right to be treated fairly, with respect and trust. We have the
responsibility to respect our peers, the staff, and guests of our school.

We have the right to a safe learning environment, with participation for
all. We have the responsibility to maintain our self-control and be
responsible for our actions.

We have the right to celebrate our own cultures. We have the
responsibility to respect the cultures of others.

THIS IS THE FAIR AND SAFE WAY.

Atlantic Memorial-Terence Bay Elementary School

3591 Prospect Rd
White's Lake, Nova Scotia
B3T 1Z3 • 902-852-2166

Terence Bay has a discipline policy that reflects a proactive, flexible approach to a culture of peace. Here are some excerpts from this policy.

Discipline Policy: A Way of Being

Mission Statement

It is our mission to provide a peaceful, stimulating, safe community where the joy of learning is celebrated and shared by all. All who enter are treated with respect, valued for their uniqueness, celebrated for their accomplishments, guided toward their potential, prepared to meet the challenges of the future.

Introduction

It is our goal to maximize the potential of each individual in a positive, constructive manner. The inviting atmosphere within our school encourages involvement and support from the community, fostering responsible individuals with a strong sense of values toward self, others, and the environment. The warm, caring relationships between students and staff ensure a respect for each other and a love of learning. Encouragement and praise are used daily to help each school member achieve the highest standards in all that they do. The courteous, cooperative manner that is encouraged in all aspects of school life has become a "way of being" in Terence Bay, allowing each individual's voice to be heard, ultimately enhancing the learning that takes place.

Our Discipline Beliefs

In Terence Bay We Believe:

Respect is a reflection of a value system where individuals express dignity, honesty, self-esteem, and consideration for self, others, and the environment that we all share.

Rules are a commonly agreed upon set of expectations that provide an environment that is peaceful and respectful to all.

Punishments are behaviors toward others with the purpose of controlling, belittling, or causing pain for wrong doings. In Terence Bay School, we do not value, practice, or condone the use of punishment.

Consistency is the act of keeping to the same common understanding, while applying the established code of behavior.

Consequences are the logical results of behaviors.

Discipline, which is developed throughout life, enables one to govern one's behavior in all situations.

Responsible behavior is a way of acting in a committed, mature, trustworthy fashion, which reflects awareness of expectations and the consequences associated with one's actions.

Proactive Measures

We, in Terence Bay, believe and have found that student behavior problems will be infrequent, as individuals know daily that they are loved, respected, and aware of expectations. We celebrate success daily, report on positive accomplishments, and use effective and affective praise. Also, involvement of the children in establishing classroom behavior guidelines based on self-esteem and mutual respect is an essential element. Thus, limited time and effort should be needed in corrective action.

The motto should not be, "Forgive one another." Rather it should be, "Understand one another."

—Emma Goldman

Our expectations of behavior are that we are courteous, considerate, respectful, thoughtful, and responsible of school guidelines in place in our classrooms, school, and playground areas. Most members of the school community at all times assume responsibility for actions and show appropriate behavior and healthy, positive attitudes.

We are consistently encouraging behaviors and ways of being that:

- increase the potential for students to achieve in school
- promote good will and harmony among all members of the school community
- increase the potential for the student to be an active, contributing member of society
- foster a peaceful, inviting environment

Our Terence Bay community has proactively valued, respected, and celebrated all members through:

- positive greetings to all who visit
- joint newsletters featuring children's work
- workshops
- communicating expectations to parents
- 1-2-3-Magic
- Home and School Association
- peer helper training

- Code of Behavior—posted, reviewed, updated
- monthly self-esteem focus
- safety promotion and procedures
- Second Step®
- positive language and procedures
- celebrity lunches
- supporting each other consistently
- valuing others—seniors as guests
- students as patrollers
- responsibilities for children
- co-op discipline workshop
- peace tables
- peer mediation
- peaceful objectives
- welcoming atmosphere
- prominent displays of children's work
- many books created by children in library
- calendars and cards promoting children's work

Bel Ayr Elementary School

4 Bell Street
Dartmouth, Nova Scotia
B2W 2P3 • 902-435-8360

Discipline Policy

Mission Statement

Bel Ayr Elementary School is dedicated to developing the full potential of all students academically, socially, and emotionally by providing dynamic and diverse educational opportunities in a safe, nurturing, and positive environment.

Philosophy of Discipline

Discipline is an educational process that develops and promotes the growth of students' self-control, encourages and reinforces responsible behavior. Discipline involves reasonable rules, logical consequences, and consistent application of these rules and consequences.

Beliefs

1. Discipline encourages positive choices, cooperation, and proper ownership of problems.

2. Discipline offers the opportunity to grow in responsibility, providing students with logical consequences for their mistakes.

3. Discipline is a shared responsibility involving students, teachers, parents, guardians, and community.

4. Discipline must be fair, equitable, and yet flexible without undermining the credibility of the policy.

Student Expectations and Responsibilities

It is expected that:

1. Students will be safe at Bel Ayr and when traveling to and from school.

   It is the student's responsibility not to tease, threaten, or physically harm anyone (adults and peers) at school or en route to and from school.

2. A quality education will be provided for the students at Bel Ayr free from bias, prejudice, and intolerance.

   Students have the responsibility to pay attention to instruction, work cooperatively, complete assignments, and follow established classroom guidelines.

3. Students will be treated with respect and courtesy by peers and adults.

   Students have the responsibility to treat all adults and peers with respect and courtesy, remembering not to name-call, be verbally abusive, or use inappropriate language.

4. Students will be able to express their point of view in an appropriate place and time.

   Students have the responsibility not to talk, interrupt, shout, or make loud noises when others are speaking and/or working.

5. Students will have a school environment free from litter, graffiti, and defaced school property.

   Students have the responsibility to respect school property by not littering or defacing property.

Code of Behavior

Appropriate Behaviors:

- Prepared for class (homework completed, materials ready, and so on)
- Respect all staff, guests, fellow students, and the school
- Demonstrate "I Care" language
- Practice "Peacemaking" skills
- Promote a spirit of cooperation and excellence
- Respect individual classroom and school rules
- Walk quietly in halls and classrooms

Appropriate Behaviors May Lead to Any of These Consequences:

- Smile or handshake
- Positive comment, verbal or written
- Glad note or positive phone call home
- An atmosphere that promotes self-esteem
- Appropriate role modeling

Inappropriate Behaviors:

- Disruption in class
- Saucy, inappropriate remarks
- Profane language
- Bullying, name-calling, pushing, or rough play
- Defacement of school or personal property
- Racial slurs (racist behavior)

Inappropriate Behaviors May Lead to Any of These Consequences:

- Mediation (by peers, teacher, or principal)
- Consultation with parents
- Time out
- Detention
- Warning letter
- Suspension (following proper procedures)
- Clean, repair, and/or replace damaged property

A Parent's Code of Ethics

I will establish a direct and personal contact with my child's school by visiting it and getting firsthand knowledge of its teaching activities and facilities.

I will demonstrate constructive attitudes toward school and its programs by supporting and cooperating with the teaching staff and the school board to the fullest extent.

I will make no criticism of the school without ensuring that I have accurate and firsthand information.

I will encourage a positive attitude on the part of my child and will refrain from criticism of the teachers or school in her/his presence.

I will expect nothing for myself or for my child that is contrary to the interests of the entire school.

I will accept my share of the responsibility for the partnership between home and school in the education of my child.

I will cooperate with the school in developing and protecting the health and character of children.

I will seek to learn about education materials and methods so that I better understand my child's school.

Yorkdale Central School

270 Gladstone Ave. S.
Yorkton, Saskatchewan
S3N 3C6 • 306-783-5412

Mission Statement

Yorkdale's mission statement is clear about its focus: "At Yorkdale
Central School, together with our parents and community, we are
committed to providing a caring, peaceful community."

Principal Morley Maier expresses his belief in the importance of
relationships and attitude. "This is not really about programs. It's about
a firm belief that children deserve to be nurtured and protected."

At Yorkdale, several initiatives contribute to the peaceful climate in the
school.

Violence Awareness and Prevention Program

Community organizations, together with school staff, help grade-seven
students become more aware of issues related to violence. Three specific
goals have been established for this program:

1. Students learn what violence is and develop an awareness of different
   kinds of violence.

2. Students learn which community agencies and programs help both the
   victim and the offender.

3. Students acquire enhanced skills in dealing with potentially violent
   situations.

Parents are involved as well. They are invited to a Violence Awareness
Evening. Here, they can view students' projects on such themes as violence
in music, movies, and other media; animal abuse; and physical, emotional,
or sexual abuse.

A Safe, Active, and Peaceful Playground

Yorkdale has made a special effort to create a better playground
environment for students. The first step was to ensure that the existing
play equipment was in good repair, then the School Division Board
worked with the Parent Advisory Board to provide additional equipment.

Clear Expectations

Both students and parents are aware of the playground expectations for behavior. To ensure that each student understands these expectations, all classroom teachers spend time with their students "teaching" the rules. Much of this instruction is done in the playground, and the reasons for each rule are explained.

Simple Games

During physical education classes, students have opportunities to learn simple playground games. In many schools, problems on the playground arise when children do not have enough to do. Conflict is significantly reduced when children engage in games and other activities.

S.N.A.P.

When conflict does occur on the playground, students are taught to use a conflict resolution strategy called S.N.A.P. (Stop Now and Plan). Those involved snap their fingers, which triggers the process of stopping for a moment and thinking about the best way to respond.

Bully-Proofing

School counselor, Shelly Westberg, together with Constable Theresa Thompson, deliver a series of lessons to help students understand the seriousness of bullying behaviors and to offer students strategies for dealing with bullying. Bully Boxes, placed at strategic locations throughout the school, are used by students to report (not tattle about) incidents of bullying.[8] School staff members are committed to eliminating bullying by creating ongoing awareness and vigilant follow-up with consequences and support as necessary.

A bulletin board at Yorkdale announces:

Our School…Yorkdale Central School

Looks like…
- people having fun
- people working together
- a peaceful school with hardly any fighting
- friendly and inviting
- visitors enjoy being here
- kids smiling at visitors

---

8. The goal of reporting is to help someone; the goal of tattling is to get someone into trouble.

- happy
- busy
- a fun place to be
- a place for laughter
- everybody's a kid
- an active place
- smiling faces
- artistic
- neat and clean

Feels like…
- a caring, safe, and friendly place
- a comfortable place
- a fun place
- an extended family
- we've crossed a river or two
- it's supportive
- an inviting and warm atmosphere
- a place where you can be yourself
- part of a friendly group that accepts the real you
- we are sharing the "joy of learning"
- it's supportive
- hopeful/encouraged
- a smart place
- a cool school

Sounds like…
- it's alive
- a happy place
- silent concentration
- cheerful greetings in the hallway
- the band is playing
- fun activities are going on
- it's busy
- noisy and loud
- a herd of buffalo at recess, noon, and 3:30
- laughter
- Mr. Stewart's choir singing

Coral Springs High School

7201 Sample Road
Coral Springs, Florida, USA
33065 • 954-344-3400

Conflict Resolution Curriculum

Some secondary schools—Coral Springs High School in Florida is one of them—have made a conscious decision to expand the traditional curriculum to include the kinds of life skills that are essential to being successful in the working world.

Teacher Kathleen Matchunis developed a course that teaches students (1) greater awareness of issues that may lead to conflict and (2) creative approaches to resolving conflict. To promote this course, Ms. Matchunis distributes the following class description to interested students:

All progress begins with differences of opinion and moves onward as the differences are adjusted through mutual reason and understanding.

—Harry Truman

Conflict Resolution Class

■ *Who* is it really for?

It is for students who want to learn ways of resolving problems or conflicts with other students, teachers, family members, or themselves. In other words, it is for anyone who wants to live a more stress-free life. If you enjoy helping others, you can also become a mediator.

■ *What* is this course about?

In conflict resolution, we view videos, hold lecture and discussion sessions, do projects, and role-play to learn techniques for resolving conflicts.

■ *Why* take conflict resolution class?

It is a stress-free elective that is not homework intensive. It will teach you practical life skills so that you can handle conflicts at home, at school, or in the workplace.

The following curriculum outline reflects the valuable concepts and life skills offered in the conflict resolution course:

Week 1	The Nature of Conflict
Week 2	Causes of Conflict
Week 3	Styles of Conflict Resolution
Week 4	Diversity Issues
Week 5	Recognizing Anger and Controlling It
Week 6	Gangs and Organizational Rage
Week 7	The Process of Conflict Mediation
Week 8	Multicultural Issues, Values, and Body Language
Week 9	Role-Plays (Practicing Conflict Mediation)
Week 10	De-escalating Conflict
Week 11	Healthy Relaxation Techniques, Family Conflicts
Week 12	Research—National Conflicts Project
Week 13	Presentation—National Conflicts Project
Week 14	Research—International Conflicts Projects
Week 15	Presentation—International Conflicts Projects
Week 16	Research on Famous Peacemakers
Week 17	Presentation on Famous Peacemaker Projects
Week 18	Date Rape and Sexual Harassment

Unity School

101 N.W. 22nd Street
Delray Beach
Florida, USA 33444 • 561-276-4414

Lessons in Living

Unity School, which I visit on a regular basis, has been a great source of inspiration for me since 1980. It is a multi-denominational school and has long been a forerunner in promoting peace. The school was founded in Delray Beach, Florida, in 1964, on the principles of nonviolent living, resolving conflict in harmonious ways, and the value of a positive attitude. These principles are embraced by Unity's Lessons in Living program. For many years, Judith Carter, Director of the Lessons in Living program, has been the impetus behind the program's success. Judith developed numerous innovative ideas to inspire her students and to promote the individual worth and dignity of each child. Every Unity School student attends Lessons in Living classes throughout the school year. It is apparent that these lessons have become an integral part of daily life at the school.

Unity School radiates harmony, serenity, and kindness. The ethos of peaceful living has been cultivated by decades of practical applications of its founding principles. For example, students are taught that true giving is unconditional, and it rewards the giver as well as the receiver. All students in grades six to eight give to the community by engaging in ten to twenty hours of community service projects throughout the year.

"I must do something" will always solve more problems than "Something must be done."

—Anonymous

Lessons in Living classroom.

Peace Day

Peace Day is held each year to celebrate the message of nonviolence launched at the school's founding. Each year, Peace Day focuses on a different theme, and all students play a role in bringing the theme to life.

During one visit, I spent time with Darlene Lang and her grade-four students. They had prepared a box of individually designed and crafted peace messages for me to deliver to a school in Macedonia. The messages spoke volumes about the impact Lessons in Living have had on the students. The following are a sampling of these caring and reflective messages:

- Let joy spread throughout your country.
- Believe in yourself.
- Say, "I love myself" ten times a day.
- If you believe in yourself you can accomplish anything.
- Dream peace.
- You can create peace if only in your own heart.
- Cherish every kindness spoken to you.
- Look for the good things in life.
- Time passes so quickly, make the best of every moment.
- I hope you and your people find peace.
- Look for the greatness within you.

Candle Lighting/Talking Stick

Classes often start with the lighting of a candle and a silent meditation. Students told me that this tradition makes them feel relaxed and peaceful.

When all is quiet, a talking stick is passed from student to student. The person holding the stick has an opportunity to express his or her feelings, thoughts, ideas, and aspirations while others listen.

Burning Bowl Ceremony

Early in the school year, older students are encouraged to write on paper a list of things they feel inadequate about or believe they cannot do. One by one, each student is invited to light a corner of the paper and drop it into a large bowl of water. Burning the list is analogous to ridding oneself of the doubts and feelings of inadequacy.

Students are next asked to write a letter to themselves describing a personal goal. Near the end of the year, these letters are mailed to the students by the teacher. In this way, individual students can assess whether they have accomplished the goal they set for themselves at the start of the year.

Scale of Feelings

At circle time, students are asked to share how they are feeling that day. They use a scale from 1-10, with 10 being the best. Students can say as much or as little as they wish about the reasons for their rating of the day; they can pass if they do not wish to participate.

Heartmath™

Students are encouraged to release negative thoughts and focus on the positive. Although this is inherent in the school's philosophy, students are also shown practical strategies for doing so. Many of these ideas originate from the Heartmath Institute (www.heartmath.org).

Each student has a small stuffed heart to hold when feeling anxious or discouraged and wants to focus more on the positive. When one student explained to me that his grandmother uses his stuffed heart when she feels stressed, it was apparent to me that the lessons learned by the students had become an important part of family life.

Unity School Peace Prayer

The students have a prayer called Unity School Peace Prayer that is an important part of the opening activities each morning.

Unity School Peace Prayer

Dear God of my heart,
I intend to radiate peace from the greatness within me.

As I… listen with the ears of understanding,
speak with the voice of kindness, and
feel with the heart of compassion
And when I meet another, I behold the Truth…

I see only Love.

- Judith Carter and Terri Stec

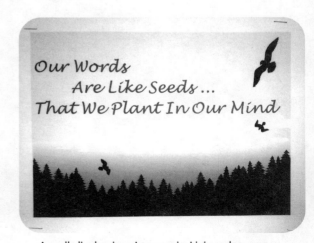

A wall display in a Lessons in Living classroom.

Unity School's Life's Lessons

These lessons are posted in the classroom and act as a reminder to students to think positively:

- You will receive a body. You may like it or hate it, but it will be yours for the entire period this time around.

- You will learn lessons. You will enroll in a full-time informal school called life. Each day in this school, you will have the opportunity to learn lessons. You may like the lessons or think them irrelevant.

- There are no mistakes, only lessons. Growth is the process of trial and error and experimentation. The "failed" experiments are as much part of the process as the experiment that ultimately works.

- A lesson is repeated until learned. A lesson will be presented to you in various forms until you have learned it. When you learn it, you can then go on to the next lesson.

- Learning lessons does not end. There is no part of life that does not contain its lessons. If you are alive, there are lessons to be learned.

- "There" is not a better place than "here." When your "there" has become a "here," you will simply obtain another "there" that will, again, look better than "here."

- You cannot love or hate something about another person unless it reflects to you something you love or hate about yourself.

- What you make of your life is up to you. You have all the tools and resources you need. What you do with them is up to you. The choice is yours. Your answers lie inside you.

- The answers to life's questions lie inside you. All you need to do is look, listen, and trust.

PEACE PLEDGE [9]

I will create Peace in my world today.

Peace begins with me each day as I learn to

- Seek and nurture peace within myself

- Respect the worth of all people and all life

- Accept people as they are, without judging or labeling

- Find common ground with those who seem different

- Practice peaceful solutions to problems

- Support peaceful actions by all people, including leaders

- Work for fairness and justice in my community

- Become an instrument of peace right where I am
  World Peace is built one person at a time.

9. The Peace Pledge is part of the Peace Pledge Project. Peace Links, North Carolina, PO Box 2592, Asheville, NC 28802.

Epilogue

EPILOGUE

From Belgrade to Belfast: Peace Begins With Me

"This idea of a global network of peaceful schools is so simple and so appealing that I wonder why no one thought of it before."

This statement was made by a principal in Northern Ireland who participated in the launch of Peaceful Schools International (PSI) in Belfast in March 2002. Since its inception, PSI has established linkages with schools in Serbia, Macedonia, Japan, Russia, Canada, United States, Northern Ireland, and the Republic of Ireland. As I continue to travel and visit schools in many parts of the world, I am more and more convinced that there is a universal groundswell of desire and determination to find effective ways of breaking the cycle of violence that has plagued so many regions for so long.

When I asked students in Belfast, Northern Ireland, what comes to mind when they hear the word *conflict*, their responses reflected the troubled history of this region: riots, Republicans, Loyalists, football, rocks, hatred, police. It is difficult for anyone who has not experienced the intensity of violent conflict that continues in this part of the world to fully understand the depth of its effects on children and schools.

Jim Clarke, principal of St. Gabriel's College, located on the Crumlin Road in Belfast, sent a letter home to parents after an outbreak of sectarian violence in the neighborhood surrounding the school. The following is an excerpt:

> The events of the past week are a reminder to us that the evils of violence and sectarianism are still part of the society we live in. There have been many evil acts committed against this school, this community, and the individuals in both. While this is acknowledged, we cannot allow ourselves to be provoked by revenge or hatred into doing something to others that would only justify them in attacking us again.

> We in St. Gabriel's are committed to a position of nonviolence. We are members of Peaceful Schools International, which promotes positive behavior in all aspects of life.

> However, it is not enough for the College to promote a view unless it is actively supported by parents and others in the wider community. We want parents to:

- support the principle of nonviolence in the school, community, and the home

- actively discourage your boys from getting involved in stone-throwing, name-calling, or any other retaliatory behavior…

Educational leaders around the world like Jim Clarke will pave the way for a more secure, stable, and peaceful future for the next generation.

In Macedonia, another country that has recently experienced serious internal conflict, I used the booklet "Peace Begins With Me" (see page 109) prior to a peer mediation training session to deepen my understanding of the students' view of peace, conflict, and violence.

As I travel and visit schools in less privileged parts of the world, I become acutely aware of the impact that a history of violent conflict plays on daily life in schools. From inadequate materials and salaries to longstanding and divisive ethnic and religious hatred, schools must deal with the effect of long-term conflict.

In the face of these challenges, the teachers I meet maintain a positive spirit and a deep commitment to creating a safe and caring learning environment. In recognition of their determination and optimism, I will donate a proportion of the proceeds from the sale of this book to help Peaceful Schools International continue its support of their efforts.

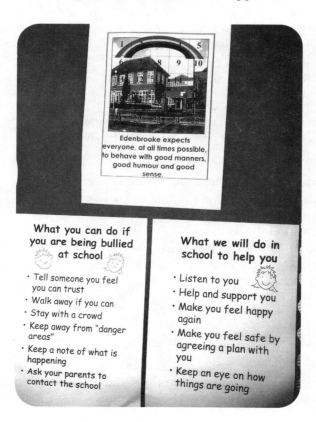

Edenbrooke expects everyone, at all times possible, to behave with good manners, good humour and good sense.

What you can do if you are being bullied at school

- Tell someone you feel you can trust
- Walk away if you can
- Stay with a crowd
- Keep away from "danger areas"
- Keep a note of what is happening
- Ask your parents to contact the school

What we will do in school to help you

- Listen to you
- Help and support you
- Make you feel happy again
- Make you feel safe by agreeing a plan with you
- Keep an eye on how things are going

A bulletin board display at Edenbrooke Primary School in Belfast, Northern Ireland.

Appendices
APPENDICES

Appendix A: The Peaceful School Planning Document

This planning document[1] is to assist school administrators and staff members as they work toward building a peaceful school community. It is a guide and is not intended to be all-inclusive for any particular school. Rather, school staff members are encouraged to adapt and change the approach as it fits the school and its particular needs and characteristics. Your creativity will provide a plan that will match the uniqueness of your school.

The Peaceful School Planning Document is meant to be used along with other inventory, assessment, and school division planning documents that may provide the basis for the overall school plan. For example, a school may wish to survey students, parents, and/or staff as part of the planning. Collecting data, referencing curriculum guides, researching the vast field of caring and respectful school literature, and consulting with others may be parts of the plan development process or the implementation strategies included in the plan.

For further information and consultation, please contact:

Bob Green, Coordinator
League of Peaceful Schools
300-201 21st Street East
Saskatoon, SK S7K 0B8

Tel: (306) 653-1868 • Fax: (306) 653-1869
E-mail: lops@plea.org • www.leagueofpeacefulschools.sk.ca

---

1. Appreciation is extended to Mrs. E. Novak, Saskatchewan Valley School Division, for providing the original planning document. The document here has been modified from the original.

THE PEACEFUL SCHOOL PLANNING DOCUMENT

INTRODUCTION

1. Elements of the School Plan

Mission	A clear and concise statement of a school's overall purpose and role of the school
	☐ Reason for existence of school
	☐ Focus of all the programs and services a school provides for students
Vision	A vision statement looks to the future and describes an ideal to be achieved
	☐ Describes where a school wants to be, what its students will have achieved, and what its services and programs for students will look like over the longer term
	☐ Called a preferred future
	☐ Include qualities of respectful and caring school
School Profile	A brief description of the school
	☐ Overviews the characteristics of the school and the students it serves
Division Priorities/Initiatives	Related division-wide priority areas are identified and may assist in school goal setting
	☐ Goals are general improvements or aims to be achieved
	☐ Goals are developed to establish direction
School Goals	Refer to section titled, School Goals
Results	Measurable outcomes to be achieved
Observable Measures	Data to be collected to assess achievement of results
	☐ Provide information for assessing and reporting on progress toward achieving goals and results
	☐ Information from observable measures may be used to increase public understanding of how well the school is achieving its goals
Strategies	Actions designated to achieve goals and desired results
Community Service and Out-of-School Experiences	Educational objectives for activities that may involve community members outside the school
Guidance/Counseling Plan	Areas and programs the school is implementing

The Peaceful School: Models That Work

INTRODUCTION

2. Getting Started

Research has shown that change can take place more effectively if certain questions are asked before the change is introduced. Some are given here. There may be others, depending on your circumstances. Taking time to consider these questions and others may be the most important part of the process.

Key Questions:

1. Who are the potential leaders for a peaceful school initiative in your school?

2. Who makes up the support base for such an initiative? Consider staff, students, parents, board, division personnel, police liaison officers, health care workers, and others in the school community.

3. What first steps are required before starting the peaceful school plan? One step is to recognize what is already happening that helps to create and sustain a peaceful school environment. Make a list.

4. What are the elements, and what are the strengths or positives of such a vision? Create a vision for the peaceful school.

5. Will there be "resisters" to the concept, the plan, or the implementation? Anticipate the basis of such resistance and how you might prepare to deal with it.

6. What events or discussions of the past can be framed as starting points from which to move forward?

SCHOOL MISSION AND VISION STATEMENTS

1. School Mission Statement

Year Developed:

2. School Vision Statement

Year Developed:

SCHOOL PROFILE

1. Enrollment   Total:

K	1	2	3	4	5	6	7	8	9	10	11	12	Other

2. Staffing

Teachers	Administration	Special Education	Librarian
Counselor	Educational Assistants	Secretary	Caretaker(s)

Other:

3. Statement of Uniqueness of Your School

OUTLINE OF RELATED SCHOOL DIVISION GOALS/PLANS FOR TERM

SCHOOL GOALS

School Goal 1

What will this look like when we get where we want to be? (Results)

What actions will help us achieve the desired results? (Strategies)

What evidence will describe our progress? (Measurable Outcomes)

Process used in determining. (Outcomes)

SCHOOL-WIDE PREVENTION STRATEGIES AND INTERVENTION SERVICES/APPROACHES FOR "AT RISK" STUDENTS

	Comments
School-Wide Discipline Policy	
Review of Discipline Policy	
☐ Peer Mediation	
☐ Talking/Peace Circles	
☐ Counseling	
☐ Family Group Conferencing	
☐ Mentoring	
☐ Playground Monitors/Pals	
Intervention Programs ☐ Crisis Intervention	
☐ Disaster Protocol/ Preparedness Plan	
Other	

Appendix B: Student Conferences

In many schools, staff and community members work together to plan and present one-day student conferences. The involvement of the community members enriches the experience and gives them an opportunity to hear from the young people.

Often, the workshop topics are based on issues and concerns that students have expressed. Over the past few years, I have personally presented at several of these conferences. I am always impressed by the students' high level of interest and participation.

Some topics to consider when planning a student conference:

- Bullying
- Good Decision Making
- Dating Violence
- Body Image
- Teen Pregnancy
- Peer Pressure
- Stereotyping
- Homophobia
- Alcohol and Drug Use
- Youth Crime

As an extension to the conference, you might consider hosting a Peaceful Toy Fair to expose students and parents to alternative toys, books, activities, and crafts.

The performance piece, "Peace Begins With You," (see pages 103-107) is a favorite at many student conferences.

Appendix C: Peace Begins With You

The words in this performance[2] piece are adapted from the book of the same name published by the Sierra Club. The organization was founded more than 100 years ago by John Muir. The Sierra Club devotes itself to the study of earth's scenic and ecological resources. Probably more ecological and scenic damage is done to our earth when peace is suspended and war breaks out than from any natural or other human-made disaster. Each of us is responsible for keeping peace to help preserve life and our planet. *Peace begins with us.*

There are thirty-two brief speeches in this piece. It was designed to be performed by a large group or a whole class. Some speakers/readers may have to read more than one of the numbered lines. Some performers will have the opportunity to act out brief scenes that demonstrate some of the messages.

It is suggested that the cast be seated in one row in an arc formation. Each speaker stands to say the lines. Speeches are numbered. Those with two numbers are said by two speakers. Performers are assigned numbers that correspond to the words they say or read. The producer will have to juggle the acting and speaking parts, as well as the seating sequence to facilitate continuity.

Katherine Scholes' words and message stand alone, without the need for actions, if a simple spoken performance is more practicable.

An introduction to the performance is determined by the age of the audience and the performers and by the occasion on which the piece is being performed.

---

2. This performance piece, written by Tom Robson, a retired principal in Nova Scotia, is based on the book, *Peace Begins With You* by Katherine Scholes.

Everybody: **PEACE BEGINS WITH YOU!** (*They point at the audience.*)

1.	PEACE CAN FEEL WARM AND BRIGHT AND STRONG — OR CALM, COOL, AND GENTLE.
2.	PEACE CAN BE FOUND IN A PLACE THAT IS BUSY AND LOUD. PEACE CAN BE MISSING IN THE CALMEST, QUIETEST PLACE YOU KNOW.
3.	PEACE MEANS DIFFERENT THINGS TO DIFFERENT PEOPLE; IN DIFFERENT PLACES AT DIFFERENT TIMES.
4.	SO — WHAT IS PEACE?
5.	WHERE DOES IT COME FROM?
6.	HOW CAN YOU FIND IT?
7.	HOW CAN YOU KEEP IT?
8. & 9.	THERE ARE SOME THINGS YOU NEED JUST TO STAY ALIVE.
8.	FOOD
9.	WATER
8.	A PLACE TO LIVE
9.	CLOTHES TO KEEP YOU WARM
8.	HELP WHEN YOU ARE ILL OR INJURED
8. & 9.	PEACE IS HAVING THE THINGS YOU NEED.
10. & 11.	THERE ARE THINGS THAT YOU WANT TO HELP MAKE YOUR LIFE GOOD.
10.	SMALL THINGS
11.	LIKE A CUP OF HOT CHOCOLATE ON A COLD WINTER'S DAY
10.	OR A WALK ALONG AN EMPTY BEACH
11.	OR A SPECIAL PLACE TO BE ALONE WITH YOUR FRIENDS
12. & 13.	AND BIG THINGS
12.	LIKE…NOT BEING AFRAID
13.	LIKE…HAVING A CHANCE TO STUDY AND LEARN
12.	LIKE…KNOWING YOU ARE LOVED BY YOUR FAMILY

13.   AND FRIENDS

12. & 13.   PEACE MEANS YOU CAN HOPE FOR, AND WORK FOR,
            THE THINGS YOU WOULD LIKE.

14.   PEACE IS BEING ALLOWED TO BE DIFFERENT AND
         LETTING OTHERS BE DIFFERENT FROM YOU.

(Someone dressed differently or appearing distinctive, or doing something different, enters, walks along the stage, and takes his/her place in the ensemble.)

15.   BECAUSE PEOPLE ARE DIFFERENT, THEIR NEEDS AND
         WANTS DON'T ALWAYS FIT EASILY TOGETHER…IN THE
         SAME PLACE…AT THE SAME TIME.

(One performer makes an obvious show of taking his/her lunch out and starts to eat it right in the middle of the performance. People on either side of him/her stare, look at each other, shrug their shoulders, and cough. The eater realizes eating is not appropriate and puts the food away.)

16. & 17.   EVEN WHEN PEOPLE ARE NOT VERY DIFFERENT THERE
            CAN BE PROBLEMS.

(Two very similar–looking children come from opposite ends of the row of seats, stand beside each other, and repeat the above line in unison. When they finish speaking, they look at each other, poke their tongues out at each other, and walk back to their seats.)

18.   PEOPLE MAY WANT TO USE THE SAME THING AT THE
         SAME TIME.

(One performer takes out a book and begins to read it. Another comes to read over his/her shoulder, likes the book, and grabs it, tearing it into two pieces—one left with each of them. The "grabber" drops one half and sneaks back to his/her place. The reader is obviously angry.)

19.   SOMETIMES THERE MAY NOT BE ENOUGH OF
         SOMETHING TO GO ROUND.

(Five performers form a line. A sixth reaches into a bag and hands out a cookie to four of them. There is nothing left in the bottom of the bag for the fifth. The giver mimes a shrug of regret. The deprived performer reacts with frustration and anger.)

19.   LIVING WITH OTHERS MEANS YOU CAN'T ALWAYS
         HAVE WHAT YOU WANT OR NEED.

20.   SOMETIMES YOUR FEELINGS OF PEACE WILL BE
         INTERRUPTED.

(The speaker's hair is tugged by a similar-sized child sneaking up behind.)

20.   IN A SMALL WAY

(A larger performer, walking past, jostles the speaker, perhaps knocking him/her over. Once recovered and dusted off, the speaker continues.)

20.   OR IN A BIG WAY!

21.   SO!…WHAT CAN HAPPEN WHEN PEOPLE'S NEEDS OR WANTS DON'T FIT TOGETHER?

22.   THERE CAN BE ARGUMENTS.

(Two performers come from front stage, far right, and start an argument. After a while, they freeze and stay very still.)

22.   THERE CAN BE ANGRY WORDS.

(Two other performers come front stage, far left, and begin to shout insults at each other. After a while they freeze and stay very still.)

22.   THERE CAN BE SILENCES.

(Two more performers (27. & 28.) come center stage right, sit facing each other, sulking and giving each other dirty looks. After a while they freeze and stay very still.)

22.   AND…THERE CAN EVEN BE FIGHTS.

(Two more students stage a wrestling fight, center stage left. They freeze when the designated loser is pinned by the winner. They stay still…very still.)

23.   THESE CAN GO ON FOR A SHORT TIME… OR A LONG TIME; UNTIL ONE SIDE WINS… AND THE OTHER SIDE LOSES; UNTIL ONE SIDE GETS WHAT IT WANTS… AND THE OTHER GIVES UP.

24.   WHEN THIS HAPPENS, PEACE IS INTERRUPTED.

25.   BUT SOMETIMES, SOMETHING COMPLETELY DIFFERENT HAPPENS. BOTH SIDES CAN EXPLAIN WHAT THEY NEED… AND WHY.

(A peacemaker (26.) goes up to the two frozen arguers.)

26.   WHY DON'T WE GO AND TALK THIS THROUGH CALMLY?

(The arguers walk off to the side with the peacemaker. The arguers mime talking through their differences.)

25.   THEY CAN TURN AWAY, CALM DOWN, AND START TO THINK.

(The name-callers unfreeze, turn their backs on each other, put their hands on their hips, then put one finger on their forehead as if thinking, shake their heads, and walk back to their places.)

(The two sulkers unfreeze, stand together, and say…)

27. & 28.   THEY WORK TOGETHER TO SOLVE THE PROBLEM SO THAT PEACE IS RESTORED.

(They high-five and walk back to their places together, arms around each other's shoulders.)

29.   SOMETIMES, OTHER PEOPLE OUTSIDE THE PROBLEM CAN HELP.

(Another performer (30.) walks over to the two frozen fighters.)

30.   HEY, YOU TWO…STOP FIGHTING! TALKING ABOUT IT IS BETTER THAN FIGHTING!

(The fighters get up, dust themselves off, and leave with the peacemaker off to one side where they mime a peaceful discussion.)

29.   THEY CAN SAY WHO IS BEING UNFAIR…OR SELFISH…OR WHO IS BREAKING THE RULES. THEY CAN SUGGEST HOW TO SOLVE THE PROBLEM SO PEACE IS RESTORED.

30.   THERE ARE ALWAYS CHOICES THAT CAN BE MADE.

31.   SOME CHOICES THREATEN PEACE. SOME CHOICES PROTECT PEACE.

32.   EVERY DAY, PEOPLE MAKE CHOICES ABOUT PEACE— AT HOME…AT SCHOOL…AT WORK…AT PLAY.

Everybody: **MAKE GOOD CHOICES.**

(Everybody points emphatically at the audience and says…)

    PEACE BEGINS WITH YOU!

Appendix D: "Peace Begins With Me"

During my travels throughout the Balkans, I wanted to collect, both in words and in art, the thoughts and experiences of the students I met. I was particularly interested in their notions of peace and violence based on the violent conflict they had experienced over the past decade. I created a booklet called, "Peace Begins with Me," and encouraged the students to write and draw their thoughts in it.

The following drawing was made by a ten-year-old girl in Macedonia in response to the question, "What does violence look like?"

When asked to complete the sentence, "A more peaceful world begins when…" she wrote: *the smell of bloodshed disappears and my neighbour will say hello to me.*

Copy the booklet, and invite your students to share their thoughts on and experiences with peace and violence.

Peace Begins With Me

Peace Begins
With Me

I will create peace in
my world today.

Signed _____

Date _____

What does peace look like?

A more peaceful
world begins when...

_____

_____

_____

_____

_____

_____

_____

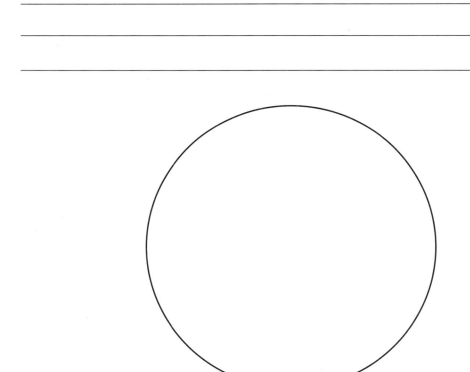

Violence occurs whenever anyone
harms or threatens to harm another
person's body, feelings, or possessions.

What does violence look like?

Peace is not a season.

Peace is a way of life.

And...
peace begins with me.

ReferencesReferences

Coerr, Eleanor. *Sadako and the Thousand Paper Cranes*. New York: Putnam, 1993.

Ginott, Haim G. *Teacher and Child: A Book for Parents and Teachers*. New York: Avon Books, 1975.

Popov, Linda Kavelin. *The Family Virtues Guide: Simple Ways to Bring Out the Best in Our Children and Ourselves*. New York: Penguin, 1997.

Remboldt, Carole, and Richard N. Zimman. *Respect & Protect: A Practical Step-by-Step Violence Prevention and Intervention Program for Schools and Communities: A Complete Program Manual and Guide for Educators and Other Professionals*. Minneapolis: Johnson Institute, 1996.

Roberts, Elizabeth, and Elias Amidon, ed. *Prayers for a Thousand Years: Blessings and Expressions of Hope for the New Millenium*. New York: HarperCollins, 1999.

Scholes, Katherine. *Peace Begins With You*. Sierra Club Books. Boston: Little, Brown, 1990.

van Gurp, Hetty. *Peer Mediation: The Complete Guide to Resolving Conflict in Our Schools*. Winnipeg, MB: Portage & Main Press, 2002.